THE GC
RETIREN
IN COSTA RICA

A guide to inexpensive retirement living in a peaceful tropical paradise.

Written by
LAMBERT JAMES

In collaboration with:
CRISTÓBAL HOWARD

Illustrator: G. Garcia

C. R. Books
P.O. Box 1512
Thousand Oaks, CA 91358

ISBN 1-881233-21-9

PRINTED IN COSTA RICA   IMPRESO EN COSTA RICA

If there be any splendor in peace, let it rest in a country like this...

The authors.

ABOUT THE AUTHORS

Both of the authors of this book are fluent Spanish speaking retirees that have together lived in Costa Rica for over twenty years. It is, therefore, not suprising that they have first-hand knowledge and insight into all aspects of Costa Rica's culture. Furthermore, during this time they have had the opportunity to gather a great amount of information based on painstaking research on a variety of subjects. This book is the culmination of their collective efforts.

TABLE OF CONTENTS

FOREWORD

This all-encompassing book is the most concise work available on retirement living in beautiful Costa Rica. It is intended to orient and familiarize everyone, regardless of age, sex or family size, with the "Little Switzerland of America". We have deliberately eliminated all extraneous filler materials that most books of this type contain to give our readers the most accurate information in the fewest possible words.

Our book is easy to understand and is intended to be used for reference as you live in comfort for as little as twenty-five dollars a day or less in Costa Rica. In fact, many Americans who would be considered living below the poverty level in the United States are living like a king and in moderate luxury on a modest retirement income in Costa Rica. They are also enjoying one of the best year-round climates in the world (72 degree average in the Central Valley) and living with the generally polite Costa Rican people, who actually like Americans. All this located only two and one-half hours by air from the United States via Miami and even accessible by car.

Don't be mislead! Other countries, even the good-old USA, are not as safe and relatively crime-free as Costa Rica. This tranquility combined with low prices and the turning back of the clock twenty years to how things were when the US was unhurried, unspoiled, hassle-free and uncrowded, make Costa Rica an ideal place to reside or retire. Inexpensive medical care, affordable housing, an excellent transportation and communitcation's network, tax incentives, every imaginable activity to stay busy and a government that goes to great lengths to make retirement as easy as possible, all combine to make Costa Rica tops on the list of retirement havens. Costa Rica is the healthiest, safest and most peaceful country south of Canada and has higher life-expectancy and literacy rates than the United States. No wonder there are more Americans living in Costa Rica than any other country in Latin America – an estimated 20,000. With some 2,500 being official retirees or pensionados. They can't be wrong!

In short, Costa Rica has both the warmth and flavor of Mexico, without the anti-Americanism, the physical beauty of Guatemala without a large military presence and the sophistication of Brazil without abject proverty and crime.

It's not too late to join others for what living was made for...PLEASURE. Enjoy this book and thank you for considering and selecting Costa Rica as your place to live. We hope you will find this book interesting, along with discovering new things, as we open the "GOLDEN DOOR" to the best of retirement living, on a budget everyone can afford now.

TYPICAL OXCART OR CARRETA

INTRODUCTION

WELCOME TO BEAUTIFUL COSTA RICA

Costa Rica's friendly three million people, or *Ticos* as they call themselves, invite you to come live and experience their tranquil country, with its long and beautiful coastlines, alluring waters of both the Caribbean and the Pacific, pristine beaches, and some of the most picturesque surroundings you have ever laid your eyes on. Many visitors compare Costa Rica to Hawaii, except they say that it is even more beautiful and best of all - still unspoiled. Costa Rica offers more beauty and adventure per acre than any other place in the world.

In the heart of the Central Valley, surrounded by beautiful rolling mountains and volcanoes, sits today's capital and largest city in the country, San José. Viewed from above, this area looks very much like some parts of Switzerland or the Lake Tahoe basin on the California-Nevada border. San José has a mixture of both modern and colonial architecture and remains charmingly quaint despite being a fairly large city with a slight cosmopolitan flavor. Even though the San José area has a population of around one million people, you always get the feeling you are in a small town, due to the layout of the city. San José or *Chepe*, as the locals call it, is also the cultural center of the country and offers good shopping, varied night life, a wide range of hotels, art galleries, theatres, museums, two English newspapers and much more. Finally, because of San José's convenient location, any part of the country can be reached in a matter of hours by automobile, we recommend that you use San José as a starting point or home base while you set out to explore Costa Rica and look for a permanent place to live.

PART ONE

Costa Rica's Land, History and People

COSTA RICA

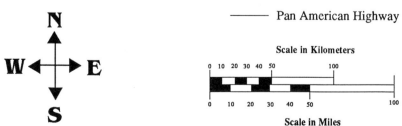

Pan American Highway

Scale in Kilometers

Scale in Miles

GEOGRAPHY

Conveniently located in the southern part of Central America, Costa Rica occupies a territory of around 20,000 square miles (about the size of the state of West Virginia) including a number of small islands mostly on the Pacific side. It is much like the state of Florida with it's two long coastlines. Because of Costa Rica's large amount of greenery, mountains, and forests it has often been compared to both Switzerland and Hawaii. Unlike many areas of Mexico, Central and South America it remains beautiful and warm year-round. This is in part due to it's geography and location being bordered on the west by the Pacific Ocean, on the east by the Atlantic Ocean, and having many towering volcanoes on the Central Plateau-combine all this and you have a unique outdoor tropical paradise.

Lastly, Costa Rica is divided into seven beautiful and geographically different provinces: ALAJUELA, CARTAGO, GUANACASTE, HEREDIA, PUNTARENAS, LIMON and SAN JOSE.

WEATHER

In Costa Rica you will be dressing on the lighter side year-round and enjoy one of the best climates in the world. Temperatures vary little from season to season and are controlled by altitude. In the Central Plateau, spring-like daytime temperatures hover at around 72 degrees all year while lower elevations enjoy temperatures ranging from the upper 70's to the high 80's. Temperatures at sea level tend to fluctuate between the high 80's and low 90's in summer with slightly more humidity than at higher elevations. Like other tropical places, Costa Rica only has two seasons. The summer, or dry season, is generally from about late December to April. The rainy season, or winter as the Costa Ricans call it, runs from around May to November. But unlike many of the world's tropical areas, during the wet season almost all mornings are sunny and clear with only a couple hours of rain in the afternoon. However, the Caribbean Coast tends to be wet all year long. It is for this reason that many foreigners choose to live on the West Coast of Costa Rica. This climate, along with a unique geography are responsible for Costa Rica's lush vegetation and greenness at all elevations especially during the rainy season.

WHERE TO LIVE IN COSTA RICA

Since we have just discussed Costa Rica's geography and weather, we think now is as good a time as ever to talk about some of the things you should consider before you choose a permanent place to live.

Deciding where to live in Costa Rica depends mostly on your own personal life-style. If you are one of those people who like the stimulation of urban living and spring-like weather all year-long, you will probably be happier living in San José or one of the adjacent smaller towns and cities located in the Central Valley. As we mention later in this book, in the chapter on keeping busy in Costa Rica, there is a myriad of activities for a retiree in, around, and near San José. Retirement is a big change for many people because they find themselves with a lot more free time and sometimes get bored. This should not be a factor if you choose to reside in the San José area because there is a large North American Colony and it is always easy to find something to do to keep yourself occupied.

Another place you might consider living is *Escazú* - a popular suburb where many Americans reside who don't want to live right in town. Escazú is located about five miles west of San José, 10 to 15 minutes driving time via to old two-lane road or new *autopista,* (highway). Escazú is one of the most popular places to live among English speaking foreigners. Bus service is excellent to and from San José. You can catch either a micro-bus or regular bus in the park behind the church in downtown Escazú. Despite being quaint and country-like, Escazú has pharmacies, mini-malls, supermarkets, excellent private schools, first-class restaurants, trendy shops, a post office, doctors, dentists, and much more. So, you don't have to go to San José unless you want to. There is also a beautiful private country club and golf course. Housing is plentiful, but expensive in some areas because of Escazú's popularity among wealthy Costa Ricans, and well-to-do foreigners. However, if you are living on a budget or small pension you can find more affordable housing in the San Antonio de Escazú area. Finally, Escazú's American Legion Post is 'the gathering place' for Americans - where they can socialize, participate in many activities and make new friends and connections.

If you don't want to live too far out of town, there are many Americans living in the fashionable suburb of Rohromoser, located on the west-side of the Savana Park. This area has many beautiful homes of wealthy Costa Ricans and is considered very safe since a large number of well-guarded foreign embassies are located there. There are a few supermarkets, good restaurants, and the new 'Automercado Shopping Center' located in his area. The only thing bad about Rohromoser is that bus service is not that great to downtown San José, but you can always take a taxi downtown since they are so affordable.

Santa Ana, located in the Valley of the Sun, about four miles west of Escazú, is another nice place to live. You can get to Santa Ana by taking the old scenic road from Escazú through the hills, or by the new highway. We recommend you check out this town. It is more rural and less developed than the Escazú area, but there are good supermarkets and some shopping. Lately there has been a building boom in the area. On the minus side, at times bus service can be slow to San José.

If you desire to combine an urban life-style and seek warmer weather, you can reside in San José's neighboring city, Alajuela, which is near the airport. This city is located about 20 minutes by bus from downtown San José. The bus service is excellent during the day so it is easy to commute to San José if necessary. Because of the warm climate there are many Americans living in Alajuela, so you are bound to make new acquaintances. There are nice parks, movies, restaurants, doctors, supermarkets, and more in this city, so it is not necessary to go into San José often. Housing is also very reasonable and plentiful.

Heredia, located at the foot of the Poás Volcano, halfway between San José and Alajuela, is also a nice city. It is only a short distance from San José by car or bus. There doesn't seem to be as many foreign retirees living in Heredia as Alajuela, but it is still a nice place to live. The surrounding countryside is very beautiful, especially above the city. There is also a university in this city.

Another neighboring city, Cartago, found "just over the hill" from San José in the next valley, is not as conveniently located as the previous two cities, because of the terrain. Perhaps because of this factor and the cooler year-round temperatures, fewer North Americans reside there. Bus service is excellent to downtown Cartago from San José because many Costa Ricans who live in Cartago work in San José. Perhaps the nicest thing about Cartago is its proximity to the beautiful Orosi Valley. Viewed from above, this valley is breathtaking. On the floor of the valley there is a large man made lake, Cachí, and park where one can participate in many recreational activities from picnicking to water sports. The lake is fed by the famous Reventazón white water-river, that runs through the Orosi valley.

Finally, if you wish to live in a cooler alpine-like setting, you can find nice homes and cabins all over the pine tree-covered mountains that surround the Central Valley. Check out the areas around Monte de La Cruz and San José de La Montaña.

There are many other small cities and towns scattered all over the Central Valley. We suggest that you visit some of these places while exploring Costa Rica in search of a permanent place to live.

There are also nice places to live in Costa Rica for those of you who seek a more laid back rural life-style or like hotter weather and beaches. There are numerous small towns and ranches *(FINCAS)* located all over Costa Rica, where life tends to be much more slowly paced and tranquil than in urban areas. If you are a beach type or warm weather person, you have chosen the right country. As you will see in our section on beaches Costa Rica has hundreds of miles of beautiful beaches to chose from . The Caribbean coast, below Limón, especially south of Cahuita, has some nice places to live, however due to the abundant rainfall most of the year the majority of Americans choose to live on the West Coast of Costa Rica. They can be found living at the many beautiful beaches located along the Nicoya Peninsula and in Guanacaste to the north. Further south, there are also some excellent places to live on the West Coast between Punta

Arenas and Dominical beaches. Manuel Antonio, considered by many the most spectacular beach in Costa Rica, is located in this area. Whatever beach or rural area you do select, be assured that life is generally less expensive and more laid back than in San José. If you are on a tight budget or small pension, you might consider this factor before you choose a permanent place to settle.

COSTA RICA'S UNIQUE HISTORY IN BRIEF

Traditionally Costa Rica has always been a freedom loving country living by democratic rules with respect for human rights.

When Columbus set foot on the Atlantic Coast at a place called Cariari, today this area is called Puerto Limón, he hoped to find vast amounts of gold, so he named this newly found area COSTA RICA — meaning "rich coast" in Spanish. However, unlike Mexico and Peru there were neither large advanced Indian civilizations nor large deposits of gold. The small Indian population offered little resistance to the Spanish and was eventually wiped out by diseases. Faced with no source of cheap labor the Spanish colonists were forced to supply the labor themselves. Thus, a sort of democratic, equitable society developed almost from the beginning with everyone doing their share of the work, and with few people becoming very rich or very poor. For a long time Costa Rica was almost forgotten by Spain because of the lack of trade and wealth. In fact, Costa Rica became so isolated and unimportant to the mother country, that there wasn't even a War of Independence from Spain in the early 1800's, as in the rest of Latin America. Costa Rican's found out about their newly won independence when a letter arrived one month after it was officially granted. This peaceful development continued well into the twentieth-century with only a few minor interruptions. The most notable feature of this process was the abolition of the army forever in 1948.

The military has always posed a constant threat to democratic institutions throughout the rest of Latin America, not to mention turbulent Central America. This is not the case in Costa Rica. What Costa Rica has is a sort of 5,000 man non-political national guard or police force that is under control of the civilian government. Like the police in the United States they concentrate on enforcing the law and controlling traffic.

Because of a lack of military expenditures that go with maintaining an army Costa Rica has been able to establish one of the best all-encompassing Social Security Systems in the world, an excellent public education system, hospitals, housing, modern communication systems and roads. As a result, Costa Rica has been able to develop the largest proportion of middle class in Latin America and a literacy rate of over ninety-percent. Furthermore, the prohibition of armed forces guarantees political stability and peace for future generations and reaffirms Costa Rica's dedication to the respect for human rights unequaled anywhere else in the world.

GOVERNMENT

Costa Rica's government has been one of the most outstanding examples in the world of an enduring democracy for over forty years. Quite an achievement when one looks at the rest of the world not to mention Latin America. Being a neutral country Costa Rica has often been compared to Switzerland because of its neutral political posture, with one exception Costa Rica has no army. As we mentioned on the last page, in 1948 Costa Ricans did what no other modern nation has done — they formally abolished their army. Also, the same year they limited the power of their presidents, began universal suffrage, and dedicated their government to justice and equality for all, thus ending discrimination and making Costa Rica a truly unique nation. Consequently, in Costa Rica you don't see any of the racial tension so prevalent in the United States and some other parts of the world. Non-citizens have all the same rights as Costa Ricans and today there is even a growing woman's rights movement.

Costa Ricans set up the legislature, judicial, and executive power structure in such a way as to prevent any one person or group from gaining too much power, in order to ensure the continuity of the democratic process. For example, to eliminate the possibility of dictatorships all presidents are limited to one term with **no** possibility of re-election.

Since Costa Rica is such a small country voters can participate more directly in the democratic process, their votes carry more weight and politicians are more accessible and have more contact with the people. Costa Ricans approach the presidential elections with such enthusiasm that they celebrate election day as if it were one big party or national holiday. In Costa Rica people settle arguments at the ballot box, not on the battle field. It is not surprising that because of this peaceful democratic tradition a group of American Quakers established a colony and the University of Peace was started near San José. Finally, Costa Rica's former president, Dr. Oscar Arias Sánchez, was awarded the Nobel Peace Prize in 1987 for his efforts to spread peace and true democracy from Costa Rica to the rest of strife-torn Central America.

COSTA RICA'S FLAG

THE PEOPLE

Besides having excellent weather and natural beauty, Costa Rica's unique people are probably the country's most important resource and one of the main factors you should consider in selecting Costa Rica as a place to retire. Foreigners who have travelled in Mexico and in other parts of Central America are quick to notice both the racial and political differences between Costa Ricans and their neighbors . Costa Ricans are mostly white and of Spanish origin with a mixture of Germans, Italians, English and other Europeans that have settled in Costa Rica over the years. Argentina and Uruguay are the only other countries in Latin America that have similar racial compositions. There is also a small black population of around 2%, who mainly live on the Atlantic Coast and a handful of Indians who mostly live in the mountainous areas of the Central Plateau and along the Southeastern Coast. Costa Rica has never had a large Indian population like the other countries in the region.

Politically Costa Ricans have always been more democratic than their neighbors – especially during the last 30 years. Indeed they should be congratulated for being the only people to make true democracy work in such a troubled region. In an issue of National Geographic several years ago, when asked, "Why Costa Rica wasn't plagued by political instability and wars like her neighbors?" a Costa Rican replied, in typical Costa Rican humor, or *vacilón,* "We are too busy making love and have no time for wars or revolutions."

Costa Ricans are friendly and outgoing and will often go out of their way to help you even if you don't speak Spanish. They are also very pro-American and love anything American like music, TV, fashion, and US culture in general. Because of these close ties to the US and just the right amount of American influence, Costa Ricans tend to be more like North Americans than any other people in Latin America. Surprisingly they also seem to have more liberal attitudes in some areas, especially the young people of the country. This can in part be due to the fact that the Catholic Church has less of a foothold than in some other Latin American countries. However, you should not get the wrong idea from reading this, since the vast majority of the people are Catholic and can be conservative when it comes to such issues as movie censorship.

Generally speaking the people of Costa Rica are fun loving, like to live with "gusto" and know how to enjoy themselves. One only has to go to any local dance hall on a weekend night to see *ticos* out having a good time, or observe entire families picnicking together on any given Sunday – the traditional family day in Costa Rica (Basic old-fashioned family values and unity are very important to Costa Ricans.). The people of Costa Rica, no matter what their station in life, seem to enjoy themselves with less and not give as much importance to materialism as North Americans. Even people who can't afford to, seem to be able to eat, drink, be merry and live for today.

Despite all their great qualities, there is what many people consider, particularly foreigners, a negative side to the character of the Costa Rican people. While being similar to North Americans in many ways and sharing a fondness for some aspects of "gringo" culture, make no mistake about it, Costa Ricans are distinctly Latin in their temperament and suffer from many of the same problems endemic to all Latin American societies.

Corruption and bribery are a way of life; bureaucratic ineptitude and red-tape are stifling; the concepts of punctuality and logical reasoning are all but non-existent by North American standards, and the "Mañana Syndrome" of leaving for tomorrow what can be done today, at times seems to be the norm rather than the exception.

Unfortunately, as in most other countries in Latin America, the custom of *Machismo* (manliness) is prevalent to some degree among many Costa Rican males. In case you didn't know, machismo is the obsession and constant preoccupation of many Latin men to demonstrate their manliness and show that they are *"macho"* in a variety of ways. Fortunately, the Costa Rican version of machismo is more "watered down" and much milder than the type found in Mexico, but still exists. There is no telling what lengths some men will go to in order to demonstrate their virility. For this very reason many Costa Rican women prefer American men to Costa Rican men because as the Costa Rican women say, "Costa Rican men are *machista* and always have to prove it. You marry a Costa Rican man today and tomorrow he is out chasing other women and drinking!" Speaking of drinking, Costa Rica is reputed to have the highest rate of alcoholism in Central America – an estimated 20% of the population are problem drinkers.

Sadly, some Costa Ricans have misconceptions about North Americans' wealth. There are a few people who seem to think that all Americans and Canadians are millionaires. It is easy to understand why many *ticos* think this way because of the heavy influence of the US television and movies which depict North Americans as being very affluent. Also, the only contact many Costa Ricans have with Americans is primarily with tourists, who are usually living "high on the hog" and spending freely while on vacation. It is therefore not surprising that there are some individuals who will try to take advantage of foreigners by overcharging them for services and goods and others who will use very persuasive means to get you to lend them amounts of money that range from pocket change to a few dollars, with no intention of every paying you back. Take our advice and don't lend money to anyone, however convincing their "sob story" seems to be.

We suggest that you don't dwell on the negatives we have just mentioned and hope you realize that it is very difficult to generalize or stereotype any one group of people. We are sure that after you have resided in Costa Rica and experienced living with the people, you will be able to make your own judgements. Be assured the good qualities of the Costa Rican people far outweigh any shortcomings they might have. We have included this description of the Costa Rican people because we strongly believe that any book about living in Costa Rica would not be complete without this topic. Finally, to help you understand the Costa Rican people better, we suggest you read the book "The Costa Ricans" that we list in the section of this book titled "Suggested Reading."

PART TWO

The Economics of
Living in Costa Rica

HOW MUCH DOES IT COST TO LIVE IN COSTA RICA?

One of the most important factors that determine the cost of living for a retiree is life style. If you are a person who is used to all the amenities of a wealthy life style, you are going to spend a lot more than someone who is accustomed to living frugally. But either way, you will still find Costa Rica to be a bargain. Despite having one of the highest standards of living in Latin America, your purchasing power is much greater in Costa Rica than in the United States or Canada. As you will see in this book, there are many factors that make this statement true. Housing is only a fraction of the cost that it is in the U. S. and hired help is a steal. Furthermore, utilities such as telephone service, electricity, and water are much lower than in North America. You will never need to heat your home or apartment because of Costa Rica's warm climate, nor will you need to cook with gas, since most stoves are electric. These services will end up costing about 30% of what they do at home. As you know, heating bills in the winter and electricity for air conditioning in the summer can cost hundred of dollars in the states. In addition, public transportation is also very inexpensive. San José and surrounding suburbs occupy a very small area. If you choose to live there, a bus ride across town or to the suburbs usually costs from ten to twenty-five cents. Bus fares to the provinces are also very low (see Chapter 5). Taxis are a good deal, costing about 25% of what you are probably used to paying. Gasoline is one of the few expensive items because it has to be imported, but you really don't need a car because of the inexpensive public transportation we just mentioned. If you must have a car to get around or for some other reason, new cars are very expensive. However, you can buy a good used car for considerably less. As we mention later on, food, continuing education, entertainment (movies cost two dollars), and above all, health care are also surprisingly affordable.

Once you have lived in Costa Rica for a while, learned the " ins and outs", and made some friends and good contacts, you can cut your living costs even further by doing some of the following: Sharing a house or apartment, investing in high-interest yielding accounts in one of Costa Rica's many banks, working full or part time (if you can find legal work), starting a small business, bartering within the expatriate community, buying fresh foods in bulk at the Central Market like Costa Ricans do, learning how to get a better rate of exchange on your money, and by even learning Spanish so that you can bargain to get lower prices when you shop.

Taking all of the aforementioned and, above all, personal life-styles into consideration the minimum needed to maintain decent standard of living for a single person ranges from $600 to $1000 monthly. You can indeed live for as little as $25 a day without reducing your life-style. However, there are single people who scrape by on considerably less and others who spend hundreds of dollars more, again depending on what you are accustomed to. A couple can live well on around $1200 per month, and live in luxury for $2000 a month. Couples with both husband and wife receiving good pensions can live even better. Remember, two can often live as cheaply as one. Any way you look at it, you will enjoy a higher standard of living in Costa Rica and get more for your money when you consider that the average Costa Rican earns only 150-$250 a month.

When you take into account all the above factors plus such intangibles as: good year-round weather, the friendly Costa Rican people, the lack of political strife and serious violent crime (no society is crime free), and a more laid back way of life - no price is too high to pay for living in a unique, tropical paradise like Costa Rica.

INVESTING IN COSTA RICA

Let's review just a few of the reasons why Costa Rica has such a magnetism for qualified foreign investors. First, and perhaps most important is the enduring political stability. As you already know Costa Rica has a strong, democratic government dating back to the 1940's without interruption, together with an excellent centralized banking system. Costa Rica is easily accessible from all parts of the world via land, sea or air. Outstanding phone, telex and telegraph system link Costa Rica internationally to other communications systems. Also, let's not overlook the fact that investors in Costa Rica have equal rights and laws to protect them. Furthermore, there are many opportunities waiting for starting many 'new' businesses that previously have not existed in Costa Rica. Many attractive incentives are also available to foreigners. You can contact the incentive section of the Costa Rica Tourist Institute (I.C.T.) for more information regarding these programs.

Foreigners can also invest in Costa Rica's nationalized banking system, private banks, or finance companies. Interest rates are much higher than in the United States (22% or even higher) and there are many attractive savings accounts and time deposit programs to choose from. There are some degree of bank secrecy and favorable tax laws for foreigners.

For additional information contact:
American Chamber of Commerce of Costa Rica
Apdo. 4946
1000 San José, Costa Rica, Central America
Tel: 32-21-33; Fax: (506) 23-23-49
Coalition for Investment Initiatives -CINDE
P.O. Box 7170-1000,
San José, Costa Rica
Tel: 20-00-36; Fax: (506) 20-47-50

TIPPING

On all hotel bills a 10% sales tax is charged as well as a 3% tourist tax. In cafes and restaurants there is a 10% tip and a 10% tax included. So tipping above the amount is not necessary. Of course, employees such as bellhops and taxi drivers are appreciative of any additional gratuity for excellent service.

INEXPENSIVE HOUSING

Housing is both affordable and plentiful in Costa Rica. With the exception of downtown San José rents for houses or apartments are very reasonable. (About half the cost of the United States, or less.) Depending on location and personal taste a small house or large apartment can usually be rented for a few hundred dollars per month. A luxurious house or apartment can go for $600 to $1000 per month or even higher. Most houses and apartments have all the amenities of home: large bedrooms, bathrooms with hot water, kitchens, dining rooms, a laundry room and even maid's quarters since help is so inexpensive in Costa Rica.

For those of you who can't afford a house in the states, home prices start at around $15,000 with financing available. Unlike Mexico some beach front property can be purchased. However, you can no longer buy or build within 200 meters from the high tide line except when there is some type of existing housing or new tourism project involved. There are also condominiums, farms, lots and ranches for sale at bargain prices. You will be pleased to know that there are no capital gains taxes on real estate in Costa Rica making it an excellent investment. You do have to pay some yearly taxes but they are very low by U.S. standards.

If you do decide to buy some type of real estate you should know that an attorney is necessary to do the legal work for purchasing properly. We strongly recommend that your lawyer do a thorough search of all records before you make your purchase and make sure that there are no encumbrances (*gravámenes*) on it. You lawyer should also explain the legalities of buying and selling property in Costa Rica. We suggest that you rent for at least six months first, before you buy and make sure to buy in an area where it is easy to rent or sell your home or condominium, in case you have to change your plans in the event of a personal emergency.

To find an apartment, house or purchase land look for listings in the *Tico Times* newspaper or inquire at one of the many real estate or rental agencies located in downtown San José or better yet, talk to other retirees. If you want to save money you should look in the local Spanish newspapers *La Nación* or *La República* because prices are usually lower. You should also keep in mind that housing costs are much higher in "gringo" enclaves like Escazú and Rohrmoser. Also be sure to keep in mind that the further away you live from San José and other cities you can get much more for your money.

In Costa Rica you can even build your retirement dream house if you so desire since land, labor and materials are all inexpensive. However, you might want to think twice about undertaking a project of this type. Many retirees, who have built homes complain that it sounds easier than it really is and would not do it again because of many costly delays, somewhat unreliable labor, fussy building inspectors, different laws and building codes and many other unforseen problems.

AFFORDABLE HIRED HELP

As you already know full-time as well as part-time domestic help are both hard to find and prohibitively expensive in the United States for the average person, not to mention a retiree. This is not the case in Costa Rica. The cost for a live-in maid or other full-time help usually runs between $150 and $200 per month. Often you can hire a couple for a bargain price with the woman working as a maid and the man working as a full-time gardener and watchman. In Costa Rica a maid usually does everything from washing clothes to taking care of small children. You can also use your maid to stand in line for you, run errands and bargain for you in stores since foreigners often end up paying more for some items because of their naivity and lack of language skills. General handymen and carpenters are also inexpensive. If you are infirm, one of the above people can assist you with many other daily tasks. To find quality help check with other retirees for references or look in local newspapers. (The Tico Times, La República or La Nación)

Costa Rica's labor laws for domestic workers are very strict and rather difficult to interpret. It is important for you to know that it is the employer's responsibility to pay monthly social security benefits, provide certain days off for employees, pay the equivalent of one month's vacation pay to full-time employees, pay a Christmas bonus *(AGUINALDO)* and in some cases, pay a severance pay and all accumulated vacation time when a worker is terminated. It is best to have your lawyer help you with these and other labor related matters to avoid unnecessary problems and misunderstandings that may arise between you and your hired help.

MEDICAL CARE

Costa Rica has an up-to-date, affordable health care system with hospitals, clinics and complete medical services in all major cities and some towns. Costa Rica has been considered by numerous international medical authorities as having one of the best, low-cost health care systems in the world when considering preventive and curative medicine. The infant mortality rate is lower in Costa Rica than in the United States and life expectancy rates are as high if not higher. Cosmetic surgery is inexpensive and Costa Rica's plastic surgeons are among the world's best. Laboratories and equipment are first class and you can feel safe having most types of operations without returning to the U.S. or Canada. Public medical facilities are so good that you don't usually have to resort to private care since most private specialists are required by law to work part-time in public hospitals. In the event that you have to enter a private hospital, costs will generally be well under a hundred dollars a day. We might point out that this includes your own spacious room and often an extra bed or sofa bed so that a relative can spend the night if necessary. We know an American who spent a couple of days in the private Clínica Católica hospital and said, "The attention was first class, the food was as good as home cooking and the same care would have cost thousands of dollars in the states."

Most Costa Rican doctors are excellent and have been trained in Europe, the United States or Canada. If you don't speak Spanish, you don't have to worry since many local doctors speak English, however, most receptionists and nurses do not. Doctor's fees for office visits vary. A good private specialist usually charges between $15 and $30 per visit, with some doctors charging a little more and others a little less. Better yet, if you join Costa Rica's national health care system you don't have to pay for each office visit, only a small monthly membership fee. Dentists are also very reasonable and only charge a fraction of what their counterparts do in the states. On the average, dental work costs about 25% of what it does in the U.S. and more expensive procedures even less. The quality of the work is also just as good in Costa Rica. If you have any questions about medical fees or doctors you can consult the Colegio de Médicos, which is the Costa Rican equivalent of the AMA. To find a good English speaking physician or specialist talk to other retirees, look in the Yellow Pages under *Médicos* or look for doctor's ads in the Tico Times.

Costa Rica's health care system is available to retirees *(pensionados)* and other foreign residents. They may join the "Caja Costarricense de Seguro Social" (Costa Rican Social Security System) and enjoy free medical attention. They can also enroll their entire family for as little as thirty dollars monthly. Retirees need not worry about lacking adequate medical coverage outside the United States.

There is also a new type of medical insurance being offered through the Pensionado Association, to supplement the government's Social Security System. This plan is excellent. For around $188 a year for a man between 50 - 70 ($167 for a woman) can get a yearly coverage of almost $35,000. This program in conjunction with the government Social Security System should provide more than ample medical coverage especially when you consider the low cost of health care in Costa Rica.

Pharmacies are plentiful in Costa Rica and stock most standard medicines available in the States. There are even some that remain open 24-hours a day, conveniently located in downtown San José at the Clínica Bíblica Hospital, 23-64-22, and at the Clínica Católica hospital 25-90-95, and at the Clínica Santa Rita, 21-64-33. The Fischel pharmacy, located across from the main post office in San José, is open 24-hours a day, sometimes has a doctor on duty for medical advice and will deliver medicine and prescriptions in the San José area. Speaking of pharmacies, many medicines available only by prescription in the US can be purchased over-the-counter at any local *"Farmacia."* In Costa Rica pharmacists are permitted to prescribe medicines as well as administer on-the-spot injections. In general most medicines cost 50% or less of what they do in the United States.

In Costa Rica there is also full service custodial health care available for the elderly (men and women alike) at a very low cost. Care for less independent senior citizens can be found for under $1000 per month. Retirements Centers International offers comprehensive medical care and assistance which includes all medicines, lab work, dental care, physical therapy, rehabilitation and special diets etc. These programs are some of Central America's best and considerably less expensive than in the United States. However, even if these facilities are beyond an elderly person's means, a full-time live-in domestic worker can be hired in the capacity of a nurse for a couple of hundred dollars monthly. In addition to caring for an infirm person this worker can tend to other household errands.

For additional information contact:

RETIREMENT CENTERS INTERNATIONAL
Apdo. 2627-1000 San José, Costa Rica, Central America
Telephone (506) 22-10-55

HOGAR RETIRO PARA ANCIANOS SAN PEDRO
Apdo. 52250, Tres Rios, Costa Rica

HOTELES GERIATRICOS
Apdo. 2140-100, San José, Costa Rica

HOGAR DE ANCIANOS PEDRO CLAVER
Apdo. 441, San José, Costa Rica

GOLDEN VALLEY HACIENDA
Telephone: 43-85-75

VILLA CONFORT GERIATRIC
Telephone: 43-81-91

* Once again, to find a good physician or specialist talk to other retirees or look in the yellow pages under *"MEDICOS"*

FINDING WORK IN COSTA RICA

We have some not too encouraging news for those of you that are living on a small pension and hope to supplement your income by finding some type of employment, or for other retirees who need to work just to keep busy. Finding work can be very difficult, but not impossible. In the first place, it is not easy for a Costa Rican, not to mention foreigners who don't speak fluent Spanish, to find permanent work. If you do happen to be one of the few foreigners who is lucky enough to have mastered Spanish, you will probably have a better than average chance of finding some type of work in tourism or some other related field. However, your best bet may be to try to find employment with a North American firm that does business in Costa Rica. You may be able to land some type of job as a salesman or a representative.

Even if you know little or no Spanish, you have a fairly good chance of finding work as an English teacher at one of the many language institutes in San José. But don't expect to earn more than a survival salary from one of these jobs because the minimum wage in Costa Rica is very low. Working as a full-time language instructor you can't expect to make more than a few hundred dollars monthly. As a supplemental source of income this is fine, but you won't be able to live on it, given the kind of life style you are probably used to.

You can also try putting one of your skills to use by providing some type of service to the large expatriate community in Costa Rica. For example, if you are a writer or journalist you might be able to find work at one of Costa Rica's two English newspapers. Unfortunately, if you are a retired professional such as a doctor or lawyer you can't practice in Costa Rica because of certain restrictions but there is nothing stopping you from offering your services as a consultant to other foreigners retirees.

As if it were not hard enough to find work in Costa Rica, a work permit or residency is required of all foreigners before they can work legally. Labor laws are very strict and the government doesn't want foreigners taking jobs away from Costa Ricans. You are only allowed to work if you can do some type of specialized work that a Costa Rican can't do. However, many foreigners work under the table without a work permit. This practice is illegal, but you can do so at your own risk if you want to bear the consequences. If you don't seek remuneration, you can always find some type of volunteer work to keep busy. This kind of work is legal, so you don't need a work permit or run the risk of being deported for working illegally. Also, as a foreigner you can invest in Costa Rica and even start your own business with only some restrictions.

As we stated earlier in this chapter, Costa Rica is ripe for those innovative foreigners that are willing to take a risk and start businesses that have not previously existed. However, we might add that running a business in Costa Rica is not like managing a business in the United States, because of unusual labor laws, the Costa Rican work ethic, and the Costa Rican way of doing business. But if you do choose to establish your own business, keep in mind that you are in some cases limited to managerial or supervisory duties and will have to hire Costa Ricans to do the bulk of everyday work. We also recommend that you take the time to do a thorough feasibility study, you don't assume that what works in the US will be successful in Costa Rica, that you check out restrictions and the tax situation, and most important, choose a business in which you have a lot of prior experience.

After reading the above, if you still have some questions or are confused, we advise you to consult a knowledgeable Costa Rican attorney for further information.

MONEY

The *Colón*, named for Christopher Columbus, is Costa Rica's official currency. Despite being one of the most stable currencies in Latin America, it has recently been somewhat shaky because of devaluations. Fortunately, the devaluations are relatively small when compared to the mega-devaluations and run-away inflation that are rampant in other Latin American countries. Since your main source of income will probably be in dollars, you should not worry too much about devaluations unless you have large amounts of money in Colones, which is not advisable for long-term investments. Devaluations can be good because they increase your purchasing power until prices catch up. The rate of exchange, which is set by the Central Bank, as of mid-1992 is around 130 Colones per dollar.

BROWNISH BILLS	¢5000
RED BILLS	¢1000
PURPLE BILLS	¢500
GRAY BILLS	¢100
LIGHT GREEN BILLS	¢50
BROWN BILLS	¢20
BLUE BILLS	¢10
DARK GREEN BILLS	¢5
COINS	c20,c10,5,2-1 colones; 50,25,10, 05 centimos

You can exchange your money at most banks between 9 am and 4 p.m., Monday through Friday. If you have to exchange money at a bank do so early in the morning, because lines can be very long later in the day and you can end up waiting for what seems to be an eternity. You should always carry your passport or pensionado I.D. when exchanging money or for other banking transactions. When banks are closed you can change money at a special changing office located in downtown San José under the Plaza de la Cultura, open Saturday 9 am to 3 pm and on Sundays, 9 am to 1 pm, and on some holidays. Also, most hotels can change certain amounts of travellers checks or dollars. Money can also be changed on the black market where you can often get a more favorable rate of exchange than in the banks. Black market money changers can be found along Avenida Central between Calles 2 and 4, in the vicinity of the Post Office. You don't have to look for these money changers since they will usually approach you. Many people prefer to change their money this way because all transactions are quick and there are no lines as in the banks. Once you have been in Costa Rica for a while some of these money changers will get to know you and end up doing the majority of your transactions. There are some money changers who work more discretely out of their own offices in the same area of town. We recommend the **Villalobos Brothers Money Traders**, who have a large clientele of retirees and other foreigners. In addition to changing money, they cash personal and social security checks and provide many other related services. Their office is located 75 meters south of the main Post Office next to the Banco Lyon, on the second floor of the Schyfter Building. Tel: (506) 33-00-90/33-31-27. Fax: 23-88-38.

BANKING

There are branches of Costa Rica's banks located in San José and other large cities and in towns. The headquarters of Costa Rica's largest banks El Banco Nacional, El Banco de Costa Rica and El Banco Central are located in downtown San José near the Central Post Office. It is advisable to open some type of account at one of these banks, so that you can have a dollar account to protect against unexpected currency devaluations, cash personal checks, obtain a safety deposit box for some of your valuables and facilitate having money sent to you from abroad. Regarding the latter, you should make sure that the bank you choose works in conjunction with a US correspondent bank to avoid untimely delays in cashing checks. Warning: You should never plan to do any banking on either the second or last Friday of the month since most Costa Rican workers are paid on those days and lines sometimes extend outside the bank.

TAXES

You will be pleased to know that as far as taxes are concerned there are many advantages to residing in Costa Rica. Investors pay no capital gains taxes on real estate investments in Costa Rica. High interest bearing bank accounts are also tax free. Furthermore, you can form a Costa Rican "offshore" corporation, called a *Sociedad Anónima*, to shelter your earnings. Briefly a Sociedad Anónima is a type of anonymous corporation you can set up without your name appearing on any records. You control all the stocks in the corporation but you identity remains unknown. This enables you to maintain some degree of secrecy in your financial matters If you are seriously thinking about forming one of these anonymous corporations, we suggest you contact your attorney. Your lawyer can explain how these corporations work as well as their advantages and disadvantages.

If you go into business and choose to form one of those tax sheltered corporations all of your expenses can be written off. Even better, if you invest in the field of tourism you don't have to pay taxes for twelve years. Also, unlike some other places, a foreign retiree is not required to pay Costa Rican taxes on his external income (income generated abroad). So, you can see why Costa Rica is considered a tax-haven by many people.

As far as US income tax is concerned, you must file your US income tax returns yearly through the American Embassy. You must declare all income earned abroad. Fortunately, if you live outside the US you don't have to file your taxes until June 15th. If you have any tax questions contact the US Embassy or IRS. If you need help with your tax forms and returns while living in Costa Rica contact the local H&R Block, Tel: 31-1004. You can also call a CPA at 23-27-87 or 39-20-45 for income tax assistance or to obtain help with IRS problems.

INSURANCE

While living in Costa Rica you will find all types of insurance much more reasonable than in the United States. Auto, fire and theft insurance will usually end up costing less than half of what they do in the States. We have already mentioned the affordability of medical insurance in Costa Rica in the section titled "Medical Care." The *Instituto National de Seguros* or *INS*, as it is called, will handle all of your insurance needs. However, because not everyone's insurance needs are the same and laws and coverages work differently in Costa Rica, we suggest you consult your attorney or the English speaking insurance agent we have listed below:

Garrett y Asociados, S.A.

Apartado 5478-1000

San José

Tel: 33-24-55; 72-00-07

PART THREE

Education

LEARNING SPANISH

Although a large number of Costa Rica's well-educated people speak English and there are more than 20,000 English speaking foreigners living permanently in Costa Rica, Spanish is the official language. Anyone who seriously plans to live or retire in Costa Rica should have some knowledge of Spanish — the more the better. Frankly, you will be at a disadvantage, somewhat handicapped, and probably always be considered a foreigner to some degree without Spanish. Part of the fun of living in another country is to be able to communicate with the locals, make new friends and be able to enjoy the culture. Speaking Spanish will enable you to achieve these ends, have a much more rewarding life style and open the door for many new and interesting experiences. Knowing some Spanish can also save you some money when you do your shopping, and in some cases, can keep people from taking advantage of you.

For those of you who take our advice and choose to study Spanish in a formal setting, for a modest fee you can enroll at one of the intensive conversational language schools located around San José. In addition to language instruction, most of these schools offer exciting field trips, interesting activities and room and board with local families — all of which are optional. Living with a family that speaks little or preferably no English is one of the best ways to improve your language skills, make new friends and learn about Costa Rican culture at the same time.

Spanish is not a difficult language to learn. With a little self-discipline and motivation, anyone can acquire a basic Spanish survival vocabulary of between 200 - 3000 words in a relatively short period of time. Many Spanish words are similar enough to English, so that you can figure out their meanings by just looking at them. The Spanish alphabet is almost like the English one, with only a few minor exceptions. Pronunciation is easier than English because you say words like they look like they should be said. Spanish grammar is somewhat complicated, but can be made easier if you are somewhat familiar with English grammar and find a good Spanish teacher. Practicing with native speakers is perhaps the best way to improve your Spanish because you can hear how Spanish is really spoken in everyday conversation and learn many new words and expressions ordinarily not found in your standard dictionary. Watching Spanish television, listening to the radio and language cassettes can also improve your Spanish. Speaking of cassettes, we also suggest that if you are a beginner or have little knowledge of spoken Spanish, you can purchase the Spanish survival book and cassette advertised at the end of this book. It is only one of a kind designed especially for people planning to retire or live in Costa Rica and makes learning easy because the student learns the natural way by listening and repeating like a child without grammar. However, if you are interested in a more in-depth study of Spanish we are including a list of language schools at the end of this section. We suggest that you first check with the school of your choice for current prices.

The type of Spanish spoken in Costa Rica is basically the same as standard Castillian Spanish except for one big difference that is likely to confuse the beginning student. In Spanish there are two forms used when addressing a person: The polite form, *USTED*, and the informal form, *TU*. However, this is not the case in Costa Rica. In Costa Rica the form *VOS* is used instead of the more traditional form of *TU*. The verb form used with *VOS* is formed by changing the *r* at on the end of a verb infinitive to *s* and adding an accent to the last syllable. This form is seldom taught because it is considered a colloquial form, only used in Central America and some parts of South America (Argentina and Uruguay) and is not found in most Spanish textbooks. Don't worry! Once you live in Costa Rica for a while and have a chance to get used to the Costa Rican way of speaking Spanish you will learn to use the *VOS* form almost automatically. If you do make a mistake and use the *TU* form, most Costa Ricans will overlook it because they know you are not a native speaker. Costa Ricans will appreciate any effort you make to speak their language.

Besides the *VOS* form, you will notice that Costa Ricans frequently use many local expressions called *TIQUISMOS*, that are not used in other Latin American countries. Some of the most common expressions are: *PURA VIDA* (fantastic, super, great), *TUANIS* (very good); *BUENA NOTA* (good, OK); *SALADO* (tough luck, too bad); and many others. One saying in particular, *HIJO DE PUTA* (roughly translated as "Son of a B——"), is considered very offensive and vulgar in most Spanish speaking countries, but usually not in Costa Rica if used in the right context. You will be shocked at first when you hear this expressions used so frequently in everyday conversation. Even children and old women can sometimes be heard uttering this phrase. We don't encourage you to use this expression. However, you should be aware that it is a local custom and used most of the time with no malice in mind.

LANGUAGE SCHOOLS

Instituto De La Lengua Española is an excellent intensive program. Six hours daily for 15 weeks - $635. Terms begin in January, May and September. Apdo. 100-2350, San José, Costa Rica. Tel: (506) 27-73-55. Fax: (506) 27-02-11.

Forester Institute International offers a variety of classes plus field trips and the opportunity to live with a family. Prices range from $600 to $1150 depending on the program. Apdo. 6945-1000, San José, Costa Rica. Tel. (506) 25-31-55 Fax: (506) 25-92-36.

INTENSA has two, three and four week programs with home stays available. Prices range from $260 to $545. Apdo. 8110-1000, San José. (506) 25-60-09 Fax: (506) 39-22-25.

Centro Cultural Costarricense Norteamericana has five week courses, three hours daily for $280. Apdo. 1489-1000, San José, Costa Rica. (506) 25-94-33 Fax: (506) 24-14-80.

Instituto Británico offers a three-week course, three hours a day, with field trips for $1000 including home-stay. Apdo. 8184-1000, San José, Costa Rica. Tel: (506) 34-90-54. Fax: 53-18-94.

Latin America Institute of Language offers various programs including home-stay. Some discounts. Apdo. 1001-2050, San Pedro, San José, Costa Rica. Tel. (506) 25-24-95. Fax: (506) 24-46-65.

Institute for Central American Development Studies offers a one month program, five hours a day, for $892, including classes, lectures, field trips, and home-stay with a Costa Rican family. Apdo. 3-2070 Sabanilla, San José, Costa Rica. Tel: (506) 25-05-08 Fax: (506) 34-13-37.

Academia Costarricense de Lenguaje offers intensive classes and many cultural activities for $975 a month. Apdo. 336-2070, San José, Costa Rica. Tel. (506) 21-16-24 Fax: (506) 33-86-70.

Centro Panamericano de Idiomas is a new school located in a beautiful rural setting. The cost is around $1000 monthly and covers instruction. Home-stay and excursions. Apdo. 947-1000, San José, Costa Rica. Tel: (506) 38-05-61 Fax: (506) 33-86-70.

Mesoamerica Language Institute. Four hours of instruction each day for $80 a week. Apdo. 300-1002, San José, Costa Rica. Tel: (506) 33-77-10.

Academia Tica offers various courses and home-stay that range between $120-$180 for twenty hours of instruction. Apdo. 1294-2100, Guadalupe, San José, Costa Rica. Tel: (506) 34-06-22 Fax: (805) 33-93-93.

DALFA Spanish School offers one month courses for around $1000, including excursions, cultural activities and home-stays. Apdo. 323-1011, San Francisco de Dos Rios. (506) 26-85-84.

Academia Smith Corona offers various courses in downtown San José and Spanish survival courses for tourists. Apdo. 4592-1000, San José, Costa Rica. Tel: (506) 22-46-37.

Centro Lingüístico Latinoamericano offers intensive courses 5 hours per day for four weeks, including home-stay for $900. Apdo. 151, Alajuela, Costa Rica. Tel: (506) 41-02-61.

This list should start you on your way. There are also private, individualized language lessons available if you so desire - listings can be found in the classified section of the Tico Times Newspaper.

COSTA RICA'S INSTITUTIONS OF HIGHER EDUCATION

For those of you who wish to continue your education, university level courses are conveniently available to foreigners in subjects such as: business, art, history, political science, biology, psychology, literature, and Spanish, to name a few, as well as all other major academic areas. In fact, some of the schools listed below work in conjunction with U. S. universities so that you may earn a degree that is recognized in the United States. You can also study to earn more credits, simply study for fun to increase your general knowledge, or just to stay busy. (See the next chapter for other ways to keep busy.)

- **University of Kansas Office of Studies Abroad** 204 Lippincott Hall, Lawrence, KS 66045
- **University of California** has a one year program in conjunction with the University of Costa Rica.
- **Associated Colleges of the Midwest**, 18 S. Michigan Ave., Suite 1010, Chicago, IL 60603 has a similar program.
- **National University of San Diego** offers a joint degree program. Apdo. 217-1017 San Jose, C.R. 31-58-55

PRIVATE UNIVERSITIES

- **Inter American University of Puerto Rico** phone 25-09-79
- **University for Peace** Apdo. 199-1250, San Jose, C.R. 49-10-72
- **International University of the Americas** 33-53-04
- **Autonomous University of Central America** - write UACA, Apdo. 7637-1000, San Jose, Costa Rica 41-53-04

PUBLIC UNIVERSITIES

- **University of Costa Rica** - contact Ciudad Universitaria Rodrigo Facio, San Jose, Costa Rica. 24-36-60
- **State University at a Distance** (extension) 25-87-88
- **Univerisad Nacional** 37-66-63
- **Technical Institute of Costa Rica** 51-53-33

Of course there are certain requirements for the above schools of higher learning. Also, remember that private universities are generally more expensive than public universities.

COSTA RICA'S OUTSTANDING PRIVATE SCHOOLS

Those of you who have small children or teenagers will be pleased to know that Costa Rica's English speaking private schools are **EXCEPTIONAL** and some follow the U.S. school year. These private schools are very academically oriented and prepare students for admittance to colleges in the U.S. as well as Costa Rican Universities. In some ways these schools are better than similar institutions in the U.S.A., in that there seem to be not as many harmful distractions or bad influences in Costa Rica. Your children will also have the opportunity to learn a new language which will be of great value to them later in life. You should be aware of that the cost of some of these private schools can run higher than 200 dollars per month.

Schools that follow the U.S. schedule, September to June:

Costa Rican Academy: Pre-Kindergarden through grade 12. Classes taught in English - U.S. style education. Annual tuition $1,070 for pre-Kindergarden, $3,130 per year for Kindergarden to grade 12. Apdo. 4941-1000, San José, Costa Rica. Tel: (506) 39-03-76.

Country Day School: Kindergarden through grade 12. Located in Escazú. Annual tuition: Pre-Kindergarden $1,245. Grades 1-12, $3,510. Apdo. 8-6170, San José, Costa Rica. Tel: (506) 28-08-73. Fax: (506)28-27-98.

Marian Baker School: Kindergarden - Grade 12. U.S. cirriculum with classes in English. Annual tuition: Kindergarden $2,150; preparatory to grade 6, $2,700; grades 7-8, $2,900; grades 9-12, $3,200. Apdo. 4269, San José, Costa Rica, Tel: (506) 34-46-26 Fax: (506) 34-46-09.

International Christan School: Pre-Kindergarden through grade 12. Annual tuition: Pre-Kingdergarden, $990; Preparatory and Kinder, $1,300; Grades 1-6, $2,200; Grades 7-8, $2,300; Grades 9-12, $2,500. Apdo. 3512-1000, San José, Costa Rica. Tel: 25-14-74.

The less expensive Bilingual private schools below, also prepare students for U.S. Colleges and Universities, but follow the Costa Rican academic year which begins in March and ends in November.

Anglo American School: Kindergarden through grade 6. Costs about $100 a month. Apdo. 3188-1000, San José, Costa Rica. Tel: (506)25-17-29.

Canadian International School: Pre-Kindergarden through grade 2. About $100 monthly. Apdo. 622-2300. San José, Costa Rica. Tel: (506) 24-28-44.

Colegio Humboldt: Kindergarden through grade 12. Classes half in German, half in Spanish. Tuition is around $70 monthly. Apdo. 3749, San José, Costa Rica. Tel: (506) 32-14-55.

Colegio Metodista: Kindergarden through grade 12. Classes in English and Spanish. Apdo. 931-1000, San José, Costa Rica. Tel: (506) 25-06-55.

Escuela Británica: Kindergarden through grade 11, classes half in English, half in Spanish. $150 per month. Apdo. 8184-1000 San José, Costa Rica. Tel: (506) 20-17-19. Fax: (506) 32-78-33.

Lincoln School: Pre-Kindergarden - Grade 12, classes in English. About $100 monthly tuition. Apdo. 1919, San José, Costa Rica. Tel: (506) 35-77-33. FaxL (506) 36-17-06.

Saint Anthony School: Pre-school through grade 6. Classes half in English, half in Spanish. Apdo. 29-2150, Moravia, Costa Rica. Tel: 35-10-17.

Saint Claire: Grades 7-11, classes in English and in Spanish. $125 per month. Apdo. 53-21-50, Moravia, Costa Rica, Tel: (506) 35-72-44.

Saint Francis: Kindergarden - Grade 11, classes in English and Spanish. Inquire about rates. Apdo. 4405-1000, San José Costa Rica. Tel: (506) 35-66-85.

Saint Joseph's Primary School: Pre-school through grade 6, classes half in Spanish, half in English, $70 per month. Apdo. 132-2150, Moravia, Costa Rica. Tel: (506) 35-72-14.

Saint Mary's: Pre- Kindergarden - Grade 6, around $100 monthly, classes in English, and Spanish. Apdo. 229-1250, Escazu, Costa Rica. Tel: (506) 28-20-03.

Santa Monica Primary School: Pre-Kindergarden to grade 6, classes in English and Spanish, around $80 a month. Apdo. 53-2150, Moravia, Costa Rica. Tel: (506) 35-41-19.

Saint Peter's Primary School: Pre-Kindergarden to grade 6, classes in English and Spanish, about $75 monthly. Apdo. 302-2100, Curridabat, Costa Rica. Tel: (506) 53-68-69.

OTHER PRE-SCHOOLS

El Girasol: Ages 2 and up 32-84-96
Kinder El Conejito: 32-39-53
LaCasa de Los Niños/Montessori: 28-01-68
El Mundo de Peter Pan: 28-49-57

Check the phone book under the section titled **"Escuelas"** for more schools.

PART FOUR

Keeping Busy
in Costa Rica

SOME SOUND ADVICE

Retirement often presents a new challenge for many people because it is usually the first time in their lives that they are confronted with having a lot of leisure time and trying to figure out what to do to stay active. As you will see throughout this chapter, Costa Rica is the perfect place to retire because in addition to being relatively inexpensive, there is so much to do to stay busy and there are so many interesting activities to choose from. One retired American stated in reference to his busy life-style in Costa Rica, "That his days were so fulfilling, that each day in Costa Rica seemed like a whole lifetime to him."

In Costa Rica you have no excuse for being bored or inactive, unless you are just plain lazy. There is some hobby or pastime for everyone regardless of age or interests. Even if you cannot pursue your favorite hobbies, you should easily be able to get involved in something new and exciting. Best of all by participating in one or more of the activities we list in this chapter, you will be linked with other people who share common interests and you certainly will cultivate many new friendships in the process. Most of the people you meet will be fellow expatriats, so you probably won't have to know much Spanish to enjoy yourself. You can even spend your time continuing your education or studying Spanish as we talked about in the last chapter.

Whatever you do, don't make the mistake of not staying busy. The worst thing you can do is spend all your time drinking the day away in one of the many gringo hangouts in downtown San José. Over the years we have seen many fellow Americans not use their time constructively, and destroy their lives by developing a serious alcohol problem while living in Costa Rica-a few even died prematurely due to alcohol related circumstances.

So, use the information we have provided in this chapter, and take advantage of all that Costa Rica has to offer. Get out and enjoy yourself!

STAY ACTIVE

ENGLISH NEWSPAPERS

AND MAGAZINES

Newspapers, magazines and other similar printed matter in English are available at most leading bookstores, hotels and newsstands. There is no problem obtaining a copy of your favorite Miami Herald or New York Times newspapers or Time and Newsweek magazines. The largest newspaper in English published in Central America, *The Tico Times*, is available almost everywhere. Reading it is an excellent way to keep up with local Costa Rican and Central American news as a whole, car sales, and a lot of other useful information. Even companionship can be found by looking in the personals section of the classified ads. Pick up a copy as soon as you arrive. By the way, it comes out every Friday.

OTHER ENGLISH LANGUAGE PUBLICATIONS AVAILABLE
* Barrons
* International Herald Tribune
* Sporting News
* Sports Illustrated
* USA Today
* Wall Street Journal
* Washington Post

To subscribe to the Tico Times (if you live in the U.S.) write Dept. 717, P.O. Box 025216, Miami, Florida 33102. If you live in Costa Rica: Apdo.. 4362, San José, Costa Rica. Another excellent newspaper, *Costa Rica Today,* made its debut recently. To subscribe write: Costa Rica Today 117, P.O. Box 0025216, Miami Fl 33102.

TELEVISION AND RADIO

As in the United States, satellite cable television has arrived in Costa Rica. There are a variety of American television channels for your viewing and entertainment at a low cost. Also, there are a limited number of American channels available on UHF for the one time cost of purchasing a UHF antenna. Most radio stations play Latin music, but some play music in English.

CABLE TELEVISION – To order call the numbers below:

CABLE COLOR: 31-38-38, 31-28-11 or 31-39-39
SUPER CANAL: .... 32-22-44 or 42-19-10
CHANNEL 19, MASTER TELEVISION
CABLE TICA ....54-86-14, or 54-88-58
CLUB CABLE ....51-38-86, or 38-17-56

VIDEO RENTALS

Those of you who are video buffs will be happy to know that there are many video rental shops located in the San José area. For a small initial fee you can acquire a membership at one of these stores and enjoy many privileges. Most movies you rent are in English with Spanish subtitles.

Video Flash (Curridabat): 53-73-79
Video de las Américas (two locations): 53-65-45, 57-03-03
Video Express (have delivery and pick up service): 21-34-66
Video Movies (Curridabat): 53-50-34
Hollywood Video Club (two locations): 25-06-30, 27-48-69
Home Movie 2000: 31-43-52

See the phone book for additional listings.

COSTA RICAN PASTIMES

Costa Rica has a wealth of activities both indoors or outdoors, designed with everybody in mind regardless of sex, age, personal taste or budget. Costa Ricans as well as tourists and foreign residents with time and location taken into consideration, can enjoy the following activities: river rafting (some of the world's best), bird watching, camping, ceramics classes, dance, racquetball, roller skating, volleyball, weight lifting, walking groups, tennis, baseball, basketball, soccer, surfing, wind surfing, bowling, hiking, football, running, bicycling, flying, horseback riding, hang gliding, sailing, jet skiing and sun bathing as well as opera, plays, movies, bridge, art galleries, social clubs, libraries, museums, parks, zoos and many other activities. Check the activities section of the Tico Times, or Costa Rica today.

For those of you who wish to join a private athletic club, country club or gym we suggest the following:

The Indoor Club in Curridabat: 25-93-44
The Spa Corobici: 32-81-22
Costa Rican Tennis Club: 32-12-66
Costa Rican Country Club in Escazú: 28-93-33
Cariari Country Club (golf): 39-24-55
Bello Horizonte Country Club: 28-09-24
Costa Rica Yacht Club: 23-42-24
Spa Cariari Hotel: 39-00-22
Club Olímpico: 28-50-51

Look under gyms (gimnasios) in the yellow pages for more listings.

FISHING IN COSTA RICA

For those who like to spend leisure time fishing, Costa Rica is the perfect place to retire. Costa Rica is one of the best year-round fishing areas in the world and most certainly has the best all-around sport fishing and largest variety of fish in the world. Take your choice. Fish either the Atlantic or Pacific, but don't forget those gentle miles of meandering rivers and beautiful fresh water lakes. Remember, on any given day these areas are only a few hours by car from wherever you are located in Costa Rica.

The fishing is outstanding almost all of the time and almost everywhere in Costa Rica, except when it rains now and then, but even then it really isn't so bad. Your chances of hooking some excellent sport fish are probably better in Costa Rica than any other place in the world. When it comes to sailfish, tarpon or snook–no place is better!

Let's first look at some of the fishing camps on the Caribbean Coast that have great accommodations and experienced English speaking fishing guides.

Tortuga Lodge: 23-03-33
Parismina Tarpon Rancho: 35-77-66
Casamar: 41-28-20
Rio Colorado: ....32-40-63 or 32-86-10
Isla de Pesca: ....21-53-96 or 23-19-73

On the Pacific side, there are:

Flamingo Bay Pacific Charters: ....68-04-44 or 68-06-20
Bahía Pez Vela: ....21-15-86 or 67-01-29
Papagayo Excursions: 68-08-59
Ocotal: ....22-42-59 or 67-02-30
Oasis del Pacífico: 61-15-55
Sports Fishing Quepos: 33-91-35
Costa Rican Dreams: 77-05-93

Nearly all of these fishing camps and lodges have overnight accommodations available including meals. Fishing equipment and boats are also provided.

COSTA RICA'S PRISTINE BEACHES

Unlike many resort areas in Mexico and Latin America, Costa Rica's beautiful tropical beaches and miles of shoreline are virtually unspoiled. Moving from north to south along the West Coast you will find many white and dark sand beaches and resorts.

In the Guanacaste there are the following beaches: Playa Naranjo, Playa Panama, Playa Hermosa, Play del Coco–a favorite gringo hangout, Ocotal, Bahía Pez Vela, Playa Protrero, Playa Flamingo, Playa Brasilito, Conchal, Playa Grande, Playa Tamarindo, Playa Avellana, and Playa Junquillal.

As we move south the following beaches are located along the Nicoya Peninsula: Playa Azul, Playa Nosara, Playa Samara, Playa Carrillo, Playa Coyote. Playas Naranjo and Montezuma on the eastern tip of Nicoya are both nice beaches.

Moving even farther south along the Pacific Coast are: Puntarenas - Costa Rica's main port; Boca Barranca - good surfing beach; Mata Limon; Playa Tivives; Playa Tarcoles; Playa Escondido; Playa Herradura; Playa Jaco; Playa Hermosa; Esterillos; Quepos; Manuel Antonio - considered by many to be the most beautiful beach in Costa Rica; and Playa Dominical.

On the Atlantic side are: Playa Bonita (portete), Punta Cahuita (beautiful beach), Puerto Viejo, Playa Uva and Playa Manzanillo.

NATIONAL PARKS FOR NATURE LOVERS

Costa Ricans take pride in their extensive national park system. Since Costa Rica is not only rich in natural beauty but all types of wild life, Costa Ricans have set aside 20 % of their territory and established 36 national parks and preserves to protect the flora and fauna of their country.

Costa Rica's parks are located in every region of the country with some being more easily reached than others. The variety of birds, butterflies, amphibians, mammals, trees and flowers has to be seen to be believed.

Additional information and a list of parks can be obtained by calling 33-56-73, 33-52-84 or 33-41-60. Most hotels and tourist information centers can be helpful to nature lovers. Please note since reserves are more strictly protected than parks a permit is usually necessary.

MAKING NEW FRIENDS IN COSTA RICA

You should have no problem making new friendships in Costa Rica, but might have some difficulty meeting Costa Ricans if you speak little or no Spanish. Nevertheless, you will be surprised how many Costa Ricans speak some English and like yourself are dying for the chance to perfect their English language skills while you work on your Spanish. Perhaps you can find someone to exchange language lessons with. This is a good way to make new acquaintances and learn how Spanish is really spoken.

You most certainly will find it easier to meet fellow Americans in Costa Rica than in the U.S., because for some reason Americans living abroad tend to gravitate toward each other. Newcomers only have to find an enclave of fellow countrymen and they can make many new friends. You can't help bumping into other Americans since Costa Rica is such a small country and there are over 20,000 gringos living there permanently. This is especially true if you live in one of the areas or neighborhoods where many North Americans reside, like Escazú or Rohrmoser. Another good way to make contact with other expatriats is by participating in some of the activities listed in the weekly editions of the local English newspapers, "Tico Times" and "Costa Rica Today". These newspapers serve as a vital link in the foreign community, or "Gringo Grapevine", as we call it, and help to put you in contact with the whole network of expatriots and the services they offer.

By occasionally frequenting any of the local gringo 'watering holes' in downtown San José, like Nashville South, Tiny's Tropical Sports Bar or the Piano Blanco Bar, you can watch live sporting events from the U.S. on cable T.V. or simply shoot the breeze with your fellow compatriots. Many Americans also hang out downtown around the Plaza de La Cultura and at the McDonald's across the street, where they can be seen sipping coffee every morning and watching the many beautiful women pass by.

You have no reason to be lonely unless you just want to be. Just be yourself and you will find Costa Rica is just the place for you. Oh yes, we might add that there are poetry readings, art and sculpture exhibitions as well as many of the other activities we have listed under Costa Rican pastimes in this chapter where people can easily socialize. The American Costa Rican Cultural Center has many events where you certainly can make new acquaintances.

CLUBS:

American Legion Post 10 (Escazú): 28-17-40
Asociación de Pensionados Rentistas (provides help and
    advice to foreign retirees and investors): 23-17-33
Women's Club of Costa Rica: 22-18-15

  * For a complete listing of clubs and related activities, look under the weekly "What's Doing" section in the Tico Times, or in the Calendar of Events section in the newspaper, "Costa Rica Today."

FINDING LOVE AND PERMANENT COMPANIONSHIP

If you are looking to meet someone of the opposite sex for romance, Costa Rica might just be the right place for you.

Ladies, regardless of age you will have plenty of gentleman admirers if you so desire. Due to *machismo* Costa Rican men tend to be more flirtatious and aggressive than North American men. Most Costa Rican men perceive foreign women to have looser morals and to be easier "conquests" than *ticas* (Costa Rican women.) So, be careful to take the time to develop a longterm, meaningful relationship and don't rush things.

Men of all ages, no matter how you may consider yourself in your own culture or other cultures, will have no problem meeting Costa Rican women. Costa Rican women have an unparalleled reputation as being the most uniformly BEAUTIFUL, FLIRTATIOUS, and ACCESSIBLE women in Latin America - including Brazil. The ladies of Costa Rica consider you a joy and are more warm-hearted and eternally devoted than their North American counterparts. A man doesn't even have to be rich to meet women — an $800 Social Security check translates to a millionaire's pay in Costa Rica. It is no wonder that Costa Rican women are highly sought by foreign men. However, before becoming involved with a Costa Rican woman, you should realize that there are many cultural differences that can lead to all sorts of problems later on, especially if you don't speak Spanish well. Generally, Latin women are more jealous and possessive than American women, and tend not to understand our ways unless they have had the chance to live in the United States. Also, be aware that because of their comparative wealth, most Americans, especially the elderly, are considered prime targets for some unscrupulous Latin females. You should give any relationship time and make sure a woman is sincerely interested in you and not just your money — you will be saving yourself a lot of grief and heartache in the long run. Also, since prostitution is legal and accessible to men of all ages, be careful of these ladies of ill-repute! Many foreigners have invited one of these females to spend the night with them, only to wake up the next day without the woman and minus their wallets and other valuables.

Most single men can avoid getting involved with gold diggers, prostitutes, or other troublesome women if they know where to look for good women. The personals section of the Tico Times is an excellent place to advertise for companionship. It is relatively inexpensive and many Costa Rican women read this section each week. Many foreigners have found their wives this way. Check out the current or past issues of the Tico Times for ideas as to how to write one of these ads. One American we know ran an ad and screened hundreds of women before finding his ideal mate. As far as we know to this day he is still happily married. Taking classes at the university is another way to meet quality women.

Finally, if you have Costa Rican friends, they can usually introduce you to someone who is worthwhile.

NIGHTLIFE AND ENTERTAINMENT

There are countless open air restaurants, bars, dance halls and discotheques all over San José and in most other parts of the country. Costa Ricans love to party and dance. No doubt once you have lived in the country for a while, you will be bitten by the dance bug. If you want to learn to dance like a Latin, you can call 21-16-24 or 33-89-14 for dance lessons. San Josés many discotheques and dance halls play a variety of music for all tastes until the wee hours of the morning and admission is inexpensive or free. International liquors and cocktails are served, as well as all local beers and beverages. Also, keep in mind that many of these clubs serve food and their traditional heaping plates of delicious local appetizers or Hors d' oeuvres, called *Bocas*.

Most of these establishments are quiet by day, artistically decorated, have adjoining restaurants, have live music or a disc jockey, and have well lighted dance floors.

For those of you who want something more romantic and quiet, let's not forget the famous mariachis at La Esmeralda who will serenade you with their guitars, trumpets and violins all through the night.

WHERE TO GO FOR NIGHTLIFE - ENTERTAINMENT...

Amstel Hotel Lounge... Simple, elegant, quiet.
Antojitos... Good Mexican food.
Bar Mexico... Live music.
Chelles... People watching hangout.
Chelles Taberna... Another people watching hangout.
El Cuartel de La Boca del Monte... Good Place.
Dennies... Quiet bar & restaurant, live music.
La Esmeralda... Lots of fun here, live music.
Mirador Ram Luna... Family style, jukebox, dancing.
El Pueblo... Large complex, different, three discos, entertainment.
Soda La Perla... Meeting place.
Salsa 54... Great dancing downtown.
Tunel del Tiempo... More dancing downtown.
La Plaza... Elegant with large dance floor.
Cocodrilo... Located in San Pedro, fun.
Baleares... Also in San Pedro, good live Latin Jazz music.
El Gran Parqueo...Good Latin dancing.
Los Higuerones... Latin Dancing in a large dance hall.
Los Tunas...Restaurant, bar, discotheque.
Bar Atlas...Discotheque, happy hour.

Classic Rock & Roll...Only rock & roll bar in Costa Rica.
Bromelia's Cafe and Grill...Live cool jazz and happy hour.
Friday's...Located in San Pedro, great American style food, drink and
    atmosphere.

FULL SERVICE COCKTAIL BARS...

Most open at 11 a.m. and close at 2 a.m....7 days per week.
Nashville South... Warm friendship for everyone.
Happy Days... You'll come back again, memories here.
Risas... Good laughs here... and food.
Key Largo... Fruits of delight for everyone's taste.
Park Hotel... Always a holiday.
Tiny's... Contentment - people watching - TV sports.
Piano Blanco Bar... TV sports - meet new friends.
Promesas... Also good for people watching.
Charleston... Nice atmosphere.
Las Yuntas... Best bocas (snacks) in San José.

CASINOS ...

Costa Rica has around 20 casinos with most in the San José area and a few
located at various beach resorts. Rules are slightly different here than in the
U.S.A. or Europe, but gambling is fun to learn the COSTA RICAN way. There
are four legal casino games. Slot machines and sports betting are illegal and not
permitted. Most casinos give away free drinks while you play and are opened from
around 6p.m. to 3 or 4a.m. The Grand Hotel Costa Rica has 24-hour gambling.

WHERE TO GO:
• San José Palacio (The newest, largest and best casino in the country)
• Hotel Cariari
• Holiday Inn
• Balmoral Hotel
• Hotel Corobicí
• Hotel Irazú
• Hotel Presidente
• Club Triángulo
• Hotel Sheraton Herradura
• Hotel Costa Rica
• Le Chambord Restaurant
• Royal Garden
• Club colonial

MOVIES AND THEATERS

There are movie theaters conveniently located all over the San José area and in other large cities. Most of these theaters show first run movies usually about a month or two after they first screen in the United States. About 40% of all current hit movies shown in the United States make their way to Costa Rica sooner or later. You shouldn't worry about understanding these movies since they are all in English with Spanish subtitles. You can read the local newspapers to see what movies are currently playing. At present, admission is a little over two dollars. San José is purported to have more theatres and theatre companies per capita than any other city in the world. Most live plays are in Spanish but there are occasional plays in English at the North American Cultural Center. However, by going to plays in Spanish, you can improve your language skills. Current stage plays are also listed in the activities section of local newspapers.

MOVIES (CINES)

Cine Bellavista: 21-09-09
Cine California: 21-47-38
Cine Capri: 23-02-64
Cine Magaly: 23-00-85
Cine Omni: 21-79-03
Cine Palace: 21-38-41
Cine Rex: 21-00-41
Cine Universal: 21-52-41
Cine Colón: 21-45-17
Cine Real: 23-59-72
Cinema 2000: 23-69-97
Sala Garbo: 22-10-34

THEATERS (TEATROS)

Teatro Tiempo: 22-07-92
Eugene O'Neill Theatre: 25-94-33
Teatro Melico Salazar: 21-49-52
Teatro Nacional: 21-13-29
Teatro Laurence Olivier: 23-19-60
Teatro Carpa: 34-28-66
Teatro Chaplin: 24-17-05
Teatro de la Compañia National: 23-45-63
Teatro Del Angel: 22-82-58
Teatro Sala de la Calle: 22-66-26

PART FIVE

Getting Around

AIR TRAVEL TO, IN AND AROUND COSTA RICA

Most direct flights cost less through Miami, however there are flights from your home city to San José via Los Angeles, Houston, New Orleans, or Panama. The following airlines offer service from the United States to San José, Costa Rica: AVIATECA, SASHA, CONTINENTAL, MEXICANA, TACA, AMERICAN, UNITED and LACSA - Costa Rica's national airline. You may contact Lacsa toll-free:

```
In the U.S.A. ............................................. 1-800-255-2272
In Canada ................................................. 800-6632444
England .................................................... 014996731
Japan ...................................................... 445-4874
Taiwan ..................................................... 02-704-5438
```

Some airline tickets are good for a year, but you have to get permission from the Costa Rican Immigration Department to stay in the country for longer than 90 days, unless you have Costa Rican residency or are a pensionado. Some airlines offer special excursion rates and 3 or 4 week packages. Others, especially Canadian airlines, offer special group and charter rates. Fares are subject to availability and change and/or restrictions and may include advance purchase requirements, minimum stops and cancellation penalties. Remember the main tourist season in Costa Rica runs from about Thanksgiving to Easter. This period approximately coincides with local vacations as well, so it is hard to find available space at this time of year. If you are planning to travel to or from Costa Rica during December you may have to buy a ticket months in advance because of the Christmas holidays. However, if you get into a jam you can sometimes find space on a flight via Panama.

Finally, if you plan to travel or explore South America from your home in Costa Rica, in most cases you can save money by flying first to Miami and then buying a round trip ticket to your destination. For instance, a one-way ticket from San José to Buenos Aires, Argentina alone can end up costing more than a round trip ticket from Miami to Buenos Aires. So, check out prices via Miami to other Latin American destinations.

INTERNATIONAL AIRLINES LOCATED IN SAN JOSE, COSTA RICA

```
AeroPeru, Ave 5 Calle 1: ........................... 41-09-44
Areolíneas Argentinas, Ave 1 Calle 3-5: ................ 22-13-32
Air France, Ave 1 Calle 4-6: ...................... 22-88-11
Alitalia, Ave ct. 1 Calle 1-3: .................... 22-61-38
American Airlines, La Sabana: ..................... 22-56-55
Avianca/SAM, Ave 5 Calle 1: ...................... 21-33-11
```

British Airways, Ave 5 Calle 1: 23-56-48
Continental, Juan Santamaria Airpirport: 33-71-46
Copa, Ave 5 Calle 1: 22-70-33
Iberia, Ave 2-4 Calle 1: 41-41-25
Korean Air, Ave 1 Calle 3-5: 22-47-37
Lasca, La Uruca: 31-00-33
Lan Chile, Lobby Hotel Torremolinos: 22-17-11
Sasha, Ave 5 Calle 1-3: 21-57-74
United 20-48-44

DOMESTIC AIRLINES

Smaller domestic airlines like SANSA or special charters, called air taxis, are used for flights within the country. The latter are very expensive, costing up to a few hundred dollars an hour. SANSA, the national airline, is more reasonalbly priced ($15 to $30, depending on your destination). SANSA flies to the beach cities of Golfito, Quepos, Barra del Colorado, Samara, Nosara, and Tamarindo. It is recommended that you purchase your tickets in advance, especially during the heavy tourist season (December to May.) These flights are the fastest way to get to your designation for your money, save you time and give you the thrill of viewing Costa Rica's spectacular landscape from above.

The SANSA office is located at Paseo Colón and Calle 24. Telephone 33-03-97 or 33-32-58 for flight times and reservations. Reservations can also be made at some travel agencies in San José.

AIR TAXIS

AVIONES TAXI AEREO S.A. .... 41-16-26 OR 41-20-62
TAXI AEREO CENTRO AMERICANO S.A.: .... 32-13-17 OR 32-14-38
or look in the yellow pages under "Taxis Aereos."

LACSA - *COSTA RICA'S AIRLINE*

TRAVELING BY BUS IN COSTA RICA

As you already know, bus fares within San José and surrounding suburbs are very affordable. Also for a very low cost ($2 - $6, or about $1 per hour of driving time) you can find a bus going almost anywhere in the country. Since many Costa Ricans don't own cars, they depend on this form of transportation for traveling to other parts of the country. Traveling by bus provides the perfect opportunity to get to know the people on a personal basis, see the lovely countryside and to learn something about the country and culture. Most of the buses used for these longer trips are modern vehicles, and very comfortable. They can be rather crowded on weekends and holidays. so try to buy your tickets in advance or get to the station early. Be sure to check for schedule changes.

Alajuela (a bus every 20 minutes or so) Ave 2, Street 14

Cañas (get tickets in advance) Street 16, Ave 1-3 22-30-06

Cartago (a bus every 20 minutes Street 13, Center Avenue-2 33-53-50

Golfito (get tickets in advance) Ave 18, Street 4 21-42-14

Grecia (bus every hour) Coca Cola Terminal

Heredia (a bus every 5 minutes) Street 1, Ave 7-9

Liberia (get tickets in advance) Street 14, Ave 1-3 22-16-50

Limón (a bus every hour, 6 am to 6 pm, get tickets
in advance on holidays) Ave 3, Street 19-21

Nicoya (get tickets in advance) Street 14, Ave 5 22-27-50

Ojo de Agua (a bus every 30 minutes) Ave 1, Street 18-20

Puntarenas (a bus every 30 minutes, get to the station
early on holidays) Street 12, Ave 7-9

Quepos (get tickets in advance inside the market)
Coca Cola Terminal 23-55-67

San Carlos (a bus every hour) Coca Cola Terminal 22-34-29

Santa Cruz (get tickets in advance) Street 16, Ave 3 21-72-02

San Isidro del General (get tickets in advance)
Street 16, Ave 1-3 ....23-35-77, 23-06-81, 22-24-22

Sarchi (ride the NARANJO BUS, every hour) Cartago Station

Tilarán - Street 12, Ave 9-11 22-78-65

Turrialba (a bus every hour) Cartago Station

Zona Sur (get tickets in advance) Ave 18, Street 4 21-42-14

* If your destination is not listed on this page, you should check with a local travel agency, the tourist office located under the Plaza de La Cultura in downtown San José, or try to find some knowledgable person who is familiar with bus schedules and knows where different buses leave from.

TRAVELING BY TRAIN

Perhaps the best way to see some parts of Costa Rica is by train but this mode of transportation is very slow, tiresome, and is more suited for tourists than permanent residents. Trains connect San José with Puntarenas on the Pacific and with Limón on the Caribbean. The San José-Limón train, sometimes called the Jungle Train, makes 52 stops and takes tree times as long as the bus, but the scenery is breathtaking. The trip will cost just under two dollars. If you get tired of this excursion you have the option of returning from several of the towns along the way by bus.

The train to Puntarenas on the Pacific Coast leaves daily at 6 am from the Puntarenas train station located at Calle 2 and Avenida 20.

The train to Puerto Limón, Costa Rica's port on the Atlantic Side, departs from the station on Avenida 3 between Calles 19 and 21 at 11 am.

Be sure to check schedules carefully.

LIMON JUNGLE TRAIN

* NOTE: At times train service throughout the country is subject to suspension.

TAXIS AND AUTOMOBILE RENTALS

As we mentioned in Chapter 2, it is not necessary to own an automobile if you live in San José or nearby. You will find it difficult to believe the low cost of Costa Rica's taxis. Nearly all taxis have computerized meters, called *Marías,* and compared with the U.S. taxi fares they are very inexpensive. Always insist that your taxi driver use his meter and be sure to ask about rates before traveling anywhere. If you ever think that you have been overcharged by a taxi driver you can take the taxi driver's permit number, usually located on the sun visor of his cab, or his license number and complain to the MOPT office *(Ministerio de Obras Públicas y Transporte)* located at Plaza Víquez. Most taxi drivers know how to get to those hard to find, out of the way places and how to locate those almost non-existent addresses around San José (most houses don't have a numbering system or address). You should have no problem getting a taxi since there are around 2,500 taxis in the San José area. Taxis can usually be found around every public square and park, parked outside discoteques, in front of hotels and government buildings, and on most busy streets. If you ever need to call a taxi you should be able to give your exact location in Spanish. This way the taxi driver will know where to pick you up. You can find the telephone numbers of the local taxi cab companies in the yellow pages of the telephone book under the heading "Taxi". The Copeguari and Copetico cab companies have the largest number of available cabs 24-hours a day. Many of these cab companies also rent big trucks, or *Taxis de Carga,* at a very low hourly rate. These vehicles can be very helpful if you ever have to move any large items like refrigerators or furniture to or from your house or apartment.

If you ever need to rent a car there are major international car rental agencies and private car rentals conveniently located all over San José. Most rental agencies operate like those in the United States. The cost of renting a vehicle will depend on the year, model and make of car. You must be at least 18 years old and have any valid driver's license, have either an American Express, Visa or Master Card or be able to leave a deposit. Also, remember insurance is extra and always phone or make arrangements for car rentals well in advance.

AVIS - Sabana norte 32-99-22

BUDGET - Calle 30, Paseo Colón 23-32-84

DOLLAR - Calle Central, Ave 9..33-33-39

NATIONAL - Calle 38, Paseo Colón 33-44-06

SANTOS - Located at the Airport..41-30-44

For other car rental agencies see the yellow pages or the Tico Times newspaper for ads.

DRIVING IN COSTA RICA

You can drive in Costa Rica just as in the United States when you have the proper Costa Rican driver's license, which is required if you are a resident or pensionado. If you are a tourist you can use your U.S. license. It is really easy to obtain a Costa Rican driver's license. First, you have to go to the office where driver's licenses are issued, located one block west of Plaza Víquez on the southwest corner. Then if you already have a license from your own country, it's only a matter of transferring information, taking some photos, paying a small processing fee, taking an eye-exam, having a little patience and you will have your license in a matter of hours. If you have never had a prior driver's license you will have to take a driver's test just as in the states, but it's all worthwhile.

Whether you are renting a car or using your own automobile it is important to make sure that you always keep the right kind of documents in your car. We suggest that you check with your lawyer to see what documents are required. Also, if you are a pensionado and your car has special pensionado plates the police will occasionally stop you to see that all of your paperwork is in order. If a policeman should stop you, above all be polite, stay calm, and do not be verbally abusive. Most traffic police are courteous and helpful. However, if you commit a traffic violation some plicemen will try to have you pay for your ticket on the spot. Be advised that this is not the standard procedure. If this does happen to you there is an office where you can complain. Finally, if you are involved in a traffic accident, don't move your car and be sure to contact the local traffic police (Tel. 22-71-50, 27-80-30) so that they can make out a report.

Be sure to be very careful when driving in San José or any other large city. Most streets in San José are narrow, one-way, and very crowded due to heavy traffic. Also, the names of the streets are not located on sign posts on the street corners as in the United States. Most street's names are found on small blue signs that are attached to the sides of buildings. Some streets don't even have signs. When driving in the countryside, only drive during the day, watch out for livestock, and be sure to use some kind of map. Don't get off the main paved road, unless absolutely necessary during the rainy season if your car does not have four-wheel drive. You may end up getting stuck in the mud. Unfortunately, the only way to get to some of Costa Rica's best beaches and mountain resorts is by using unpaved roads. So be careful! While on the subject, a word about potholes. The Costa Rican government tries to keep its paved roads in good shape, but can't keep up with the workload. So watch out for these potholes and ruts in the pavement. Your car's shocks and suspension system will be grateful.

If you plan to own your own car, you will need some kind of automobile insurance. Coverage is much more reasonably priced than in the United States. You can purchase your insurance at the I.N.S. (Instituto National de Seguros) building, located in downtown San José, or through one of their local agents.

KEEPING YOUR BEARINGS STRAIGHT

If you are going to live in Costa Rica, you can get very confused trying to find your way around, especially in San José. Except for the center of San José, streets don't have names or numbers, and if they do, they are not usually posted in a visible place. People use known landmarks to get around, to locate addresses, and give directions. If you are not familiar with this system it is almost impossible to find you way around and easy to get lost. You should not worry because after you have lived in Costa Rica for a while, you will get used to this system. In the event you do happen to get lost, you can always ask Costa Ricans for directions-provided you understand a little Spanish or they speak some English.

As you know, Costa Ricans are generally very friendly, so they will usually be happy to help you find the address you are looking for. However, it is always a good idea to ask another person because Ticos don't like to tell you they don't know an address and sometimes will give you directions whether they know where you want to go or not.

Here are some basic tips on how to get around Costa Rica and understanding how the street numbering works. It is somewhat easier to find your way around downtown San José because of the layout of the city. Avenues, or *Avenidas*, run east to west. All the odd numbered avenues are found north of Central Avenue - Avenida Central. The even numbered avenues are to the south. Streets, or *Calles*, run north to south, with odd numbered streets east of Calle Central, and even numbered streets to the west. If you get lost, looking for a street sign on the side of a building and counting by two's will usually help you get your bearings. Keep in mind that the word avenue is often abbreviated as "A" and streets as "C" when you are given written directions.

In finding your way around Costa Rica you may need to know that 100 meters *cien metros* is another way of saying one block. Likewise, 50 meters is a half-block and 150 meters a block and a half, etc. . The word *varas* (an old Spanish unit of measurement - almost a yard) is slang and often used instead of the word *metros*-meters, when giving directions. Landmarks such as corner grocery stores (*pulperías*), churches, schools and other buildings are usually used in conjunction with this metric block system to locate addresses. For example, in finding a house someone might say, "From Saint Paul's Church, 200 meters west and 300 south." In interpreting written directions you should also know that "M" stands for meters.

Here is an old trick the Costa Ricans often use for finding the four compass points, that might help make it easier for you to find an address or get your bearings straight. The front doors of all churches in Costa Rica face west. So, if there is a church nearby, you will know which way is west, if you can imagine yourself with your back facing the entrance of the church.

Finally, if you live in San José, there is another method for finding the compass points. Use the volcano Poás for north, the Cruz de Alajuela mountain for approximately south, the direction of Cartago for east and the general direction of the Savana or Rohrmoser for west. This system of using landmarks should make it easier for you to find you way around the city once you have mastered it.

PART SIX

Communications

PART SIX

Communications

TELEPHONE SERVICES

Costa Rica has the highest number of telephones per capita of any Latin American country and boasts one of the world's best telephone systems, with direct dialing to over 60 countries. Calls within the country are a bargain, since you can call any place in the country for only a few cents. If your house or apartment doesn't have a phone, don't worry. Public telephones are located just about everywhere in Costa Rica and use 5, 10, and 20 colón coins. If you don't have your own phone and want to make a direct international call, you should go to the RADIOGRAFICA telephone office, located in downtown San José at Calle 1, Ave. 7, across from the offices of LACSA (open 7 a. m. to 10 p. m.). A collect long distance call can be made from any phone booth by dialing 116. Also, long distance calls can be made from most hotels. As for private phones in homes or offices, again the procedure is just like in the U. S., by direct dialing or first talking to the operator *(OPERADORA)*. The access numbers for calling Costa Rica from abroad are 011-506 plus the rest of the number.

IMPORTANT TELEPHONE NUMBERS

POLICE 117
RURAL GUARD 127
PATROLMEN 23-43-05
FIRE DEPARTMENT 118
ELECTRIC COMPANY 126
AMBULANCE 128
PARAMEDICS 118
PUBLIC MEDICAL CENTERS:
    HOSPITAL MEXICO 32-61-22
    HOSPITAL NACIONAL DE NIÑOS 22-01-22
    HOSPITAL SAN JUAN DE DIOS 22-01-66
HOSPITAL CALDERON GUARDIA 22-41-33
INFORMATION 113
TIME..112
TELEGRAMS 123
LONG DISTANCE 116
UNLISTED NUMBERS 115
TELEPHONE OUT OF ORDER...119
AT&T (INTERNATIONAL CALLS) 114
U. S. SPRINT (INTERNATIONAL CALLS)..........................163
MCI...162

MAIL

Just as in the United States, mail is received and sent from the post office *(correo or casa de correos.)* The main post office is conveniently located in the heart of downtown San José at Calle 2, Ave. 1-3 (23-97-66.) Other small cities and towns in rural areas have their own post offices which are also centrally located. Air mail between the United States or Europe and Costa Rica usually takes about five to ten days.

Please keep in mind that mail boxes are few and far between, so we recommend that you use your nearest post office for all postal related matters. Also, we recommend you obtain a post office box *(APARTADO)* from your local post office in Costa Rica to ensure prompt and efficient mail service. To apply for a post office box, go to the post office nearest your office or residence and fill out an application *(SOLICITUD DE APARTADO)*. You will have to pay a small yearly rental fee. Mail can also be received in the general delivery section *(LISTA DE CORREOS)* of you local post office.

A word about having money sent to you in Costa Rica from abroad. There are many ways to receive money while visiting or residing in Costa Rica. The fastest and the safest way is to have an international money order shipped to you via one of the many worldwide courier services, such as DHL. Letters and small packages usually take about two working days (Mon-Fri) to reach Costa Rica from the United States or Canada. Also, U. S. banks and Western Union can wire money to the banks in Costa Rica. This method is also safe, but there can be many bureaucratic delays while waiting for checks to clear or be processed. There are many money changers *(cambistas)* located in private offices near the central post office and banks in downtown San José. Some of these money changers will often cash your personal checks from your U. S. checking account once they know you well. You can get the name of one of these money changers from other retirees or residents. Social Security and Veteran's benefits can be mailed to you directly through the U. S. Embassy, once you have established a permanent residence in Costa Rica. However, these checks usually don't arrive until sometimes after the tenth of each month.

The worst way to send money is through the regular mail. People report that many checks have been lost or stolen. If you chose this method, have your checks sent to you in a security, non-transparent envelope. You can also use one of the private mail companies such as Aerocasillas, AAA Express Mail (Tel. 33-49-93), or Trans-Express "Interlink" (Tel: 32-35-44), to handle all of your correspondence and to help prevent postal theft. The Costa Rican postal service, *Cortel*, is planning to start a money order service allowing money orders to be sent from the U.S. to Costa Rica. This service promises to be much faster and much more economical than trying to get money wired to your bank here.

It must be pointed out that the worst time to have any type of mail sent to you is between November 20 and January first. Letters can be delayed up to a month because of the enormous volume of Christmas mail and the fact that postal workers are on vacation during part of the month of December. Also, you should avoid having anything larger than a letter or a magazine sent to you in Costa Rica. Any item bigger than this will be sent to the customs warehouse *(ADUANA)* and it will take you several trips to get it out. You, most certainly, will have to pay an exorbitant duty equivalent to the value of the item plus the mailing cost combined.

PART SEVEN

Lodging and Cuisine

HOTELS

While exploring Costa Rica or looking for an apartment, house or some other type of permanent residence, you may choose to stay at one of the many hotels listed below. We have tried to list a wide range of accommodations to select from, taking all personal tastes and budgets into consideration.

EXCELLENT HOTELS
(Located downtown or near downtown San José.)

AMBASADOR - Moderately priced 21-81-55
BALMORAL - Moderately priced 22-50-22
CARIARI HOTEL - Expensive, has a golf course 39-00-22
COROBICI - Expensive 32-81-22
EUROPA - Moderately priced 22-12-22
GRAN HOTEL COSTA RICA - Moderately priced 21-40-00
HOTEL AUROLA HOLIDAY INN - Expensive 33-72-33
HOTEL PRESIDENT - Moderately priced 22-20-34
IRAZU - Moderately priced 32--48-11
SAN JOSE PALACIO - Expensive, newest hotel.....................20-20-34

NICE HOTELS
(Located downtown or near downtown San José.)

AMSTEL - A fair price 22-46-22
BOUGAINVILLEA - A fair price 33-66-22
DON CARLOS - A fair price 21-67-07
GRAN VIA - A fair price...22-77-37
TENNIS CLUB - A fair price 32-12-66

APARTHOTELS
(Located downtown or near downtown San José.
Some with kitchens, telephones and televisions available)

APARTAMENTOS SCOTLAND - Weekly or monthly 23-08-33
CASTILLA - Moderately low priced 22-21-13
D'GALAH - Moderately low priced ....34-17-43 or 53-75-39
DON CARLOS - Moderately low priced 21-67-07
EL CONQUISTADOR - Moderately low priced 25-30-22
LAMM - Moderately low priced 21-49-20
NAPOLEON - Moderately low priced 23-32-52
RANGO - Moderately low priced...22-04-55

MORE AFORDABLE PLACES TO STAY
(Located downtown or near downtown San José.
Clean safe rooms - some with meals.)

CASA MARIA DE ESCAZU - Low priced 28-22-70
CASA MARIA DE MORAVIA - Low priced 28-22-70
COSTA RICA INN - Low priced 22-52-03
DIPLOMAT - Low priced 21-81-33
FORTUNA - Low priced 23-53-44
GALILEA - Low priced 33-69-25
HOTEL ALAMEDA - Low priced 21-30-45
PETIT HOTEL - Reasonably priced 33-07-66
PICO BLANCO - Low priced 28-31-97
POSADA PEGASUS - Low priced 28-41-96
PLAZA - Low priced 22-55-33
RITZ - Low priced 22-41-03

INEXPENSIVE PLACES TO STAY
(Located downtown or near downtown San José.
* Private baths; ** Some shared)

* ** ASTORIA - The lowest priced 21-21-72
   BELLAVISTA - The lowest priced 23-00-95
** BORUCA - The lowest priced 23-00-16
* CAPITAL - The lowest priced 21-84-97
* CENTRAL - The lowest priced 21-27-67
* CORCORI - The lowest priced 33-00-81
* GRAN HOTEL CENTRAL AMERICA - Good for
   the handicapped 21-33-62
* ** MARLIN - The lowest priced 33-32-12
   MORAZAN - The lowest priced 21-90-83
   MUSOC - Low priced, next to bus station 22-94-3
** TROY'S HOTEL - Located one block east of museum 22-67-56

BED & BREAKFAST
(Small, quaint, and generally, but not necessarily inexpensive,
located downtown or near downtown San José)

DUNN INN - The best of this group 22-32-32
HOTEL SAN TOMAS 55-04-48
GARDEN COURT HOTEL 55-47-66
PENSION DE LA CUESTA 55-28-96
POSADA PEGASUS: ESCAZU 28-41-96
LINDA VISTA LODGE: ESCAZU 28-51-99

GRAN HOTEL COSTA RICA

RESTAURANTS

There are many excellent restaurants that serve a wide variety of international foods located all over the San José area. Most of these restaurants are very affordable when compared to similar establishments in the United States. It should be of some comfort to you to know that Costa Rican restaurants are clean and health codes are strictly enforced by the Ministerio de Salud (Health Department). For your convenience we have included a list of our favorite places to eat but are sure you will discover many on your own or by word of mouth once you have lived in Costa Rica for a while. Although Costa Rica's atmosphere is casual, some of the finer restaurants may require more formal attire, so you should check in advance if you are not sure about what you should wear.

Here are some of San José's most popular dining establishments. Prices vary but in general most are reasonable:

AMSTEL HOTEL: (different cuisines) 33-66-22
BALCON DE EUROPA: (Italian cuisine) 21-48-41
BEIRUT: (Middle East specialties) 57-18-08
CHALET SUIZO: (different cuisines) 22-31-18
FLOR DE LOTO: (Hunan & Szechuan Chinese) 32-46-52
LOS ANTOJITOS: (several locations) Mexican food 22-90-86
LA PRINCESA MARINA: (inexpensive seafood) Savana Oeste 32-04-81
LOBSTER INN: (seafood, expensive) 23-85-94
LA FUENTE DE MARISCOS: (seafood) 31-06-31
L'ILE: (French) 22-42-41
LA MASIA DE TRIQUELL: (Spanish) 21-50-73
LA NUEVA CHINA: (Chinese) 24-44-78
PAPRIKA: (rich tasting food) 25-89-71
PICCOLA ROMA: (Italian) 23-10-73
VALERIO'S: (Pizza & Lasagne) 25-08-38
VIA VENETO: (Italian) 34-28-98

MORE AFFORDABLE DINING...

CAFE DEL TEATRO NACIONAL: Reasonable prices.
CHARLEY'S BAR AND GRILL: Cajun and North American food.
CHIPS: International food - Plaza de la Cultura.
CONFETTI'S: Nice cafe located across from the Plaza de La Democracia.
JAPPYS: Great desserts.
LA SODA TAPIA: Best breakfasts in San José.
LA CASA DEL ANGEL: Pizza & coffee, inexpensive.
LAS TUNAS: Barbequed beef, seafood, Mexican food and a discotheque next door.
MACCHU PICHU: Peruvian dishes.
MANOLO'S: Good food.

MIRO'S BISTRO: Italian and American.
PIZZA METRO: Unique pizza, downtown, 23-03-06.
PIPO'S: Great Sandwiches.
SODA CENTRAL: Excellent chicken.
SODA PALACE: In the heart of San José.
SPOON: Best of desserts (three locations.)
TEQUILA WILLY'S: Good Tex-Mex food, fun.

VEGETARIAN EATERIES
DON SOL: Complete cuisine.
LA MACROBIOTICA: Good food.
LA MAZORCA: Great macrobiotic lunches.
EL MORDISCO: Newest veggie cafe in town.
SHAKTI: Vegetarian goodies

FAST FOOD & TAKE OUT
PIZZA HUT (Home delivery available)
    Plaza del Sol 53-36-36
    La California 55-28-28
    Rohrmoser 20-18-18
    Escazú 28-98-98
DOMINO PIZZA (Home delivery only)
    San Pedro 25-30-30
    Centro Comercial Los Anonos 28-95-95
KENTUCKY FRIED CHICKEN
    Paseo Colón 22-37-95
    Ave Ctl, C 31, Los Yoses..........25-98-12
    Avenida Segunda 21-83-97
McDONALD'S
Plaza de La Cultura	Parque de La Paz
Sabana Sur	Plaza del Sol
Av Ctl, C4 (downtown)	
TACO BELL
San Pedro	La Plaza de La Cultura
BURGER KING
San Pedro	Sabana Norte (North)
Parque Central	Diagonal al Edificio de Cristal

PART EIGHT

Red Tape

DEALING WITH BUREAUCRACY AND OTHER RELATED MATTERS

Just as in the rest of Latin America, Costa Rica is plagued by an inefficient bureaucratic system, when compared to U. S. standards. This situation is exaggerated by the Latin American temperament, seemingly lackadaisical attitude of most bureaucrats, and the generally slower pace of life south of the border. The concept of time is much different than in the U. S. or Canada. When you hear someone say that something will be done *"ahorita"*, which literally means right now, you can really expect it to take anywhere from a few minutes to a week, or maybe never. It is not unusual to have to wait in lines for hours in banks and government offices and experience many other unnecessary delays that would almost never occur under similar circumstances in the U. S. This situation can prove to be very frustrating for foreigners, who are used to fast, efficient service, and it can be especially irritating if you don't speak good Spanish. Since very few people that work in the above offices seem to speak fluent English and most North Americans have little knowledge of spoken Spanish, it is advisable to study some basic Spanish. However, if the language proves to be an obstacle at first, we recommend you use a competent bilingual lawyer or see if the Pensionado Association can help you deal with Costa Rica's bureaucracy. Above all, just learn to be more patient than normal and remember in Costa Rica, just as in the rest of Latin America, you can get the best results from people if you do not push or pressure them.

A few words of caution - There are some individuals, that are sometimes called *chorizeros* in popular jargon, who try to pass themselves off as lawyers or who will try to befriend you and offer to help you with red tape, claiming that they can short cut the bureaucratic system because of their contacts. A general rule of thumb is to avoid such individuals or you will end up losing valuable time, run the risk of acquiring forged documents, will most certainly lose money, and experience a lot of grief. Also, since bribery is an institution in most Latin American countries and the majority of government employees are under-paid, some people will advise you to pay extra money to speed up paper work or circumvent normal channels. This practice of bribery is illegal and not recommended for foreigners, since they can be deported for breaking the law. However, in some instances it may be necessary to pay extra money to get things done. Use your own discretion in such matters.

Finally, while we are on the subject of bureaucracy, all persons planning to live or retire in Costa Rica should know that the American Embassy, located in the San José suburb of Pavas, can help with the following: Social Security and Veterans benefits, getting documents notarized, obtaining a new U. S. passport, registering the births of your children abroad, getting a U.S. visa for your spouse - if you chose to marry a Costa Rican, obtaining an absentee ballot to vote in U.S. elections and U.S. income tax forms and information. We would like to point out that if you get into any kind of legal trouble in Costa Rica, you should not expect too much help from the U.S. Embassy.

HOW TO BECOME A PENSIONADO IN COSTA RICA - PENSIONADO AND RENTISTA STATUS

Recently the pensionado law was changed eliminating many of the tax privileges that foreign retirees have enjoyed since 1964. Under the old system foreigners with official PENSIONADO (permanent retiree) status, were required to reside in the country for four months a year, and were entitled to the following perks: Permanent residency without immigration hastles; all the privileges of a Costa Rican citizen, except the right to vote and work for hire; one of each duty free major appliance such as a refrigerator, a stove, a microwave, a television, a washer and dryer, and many unlimited personal household goods. Pensionados were also permitted to bring a new car into the country every five years without having to pay normal duties, provided it was worth less than $16,000.00. Now the two most worthwhile exonerations have been eliminated: Low taxes on an imported cars and duty free household goods. From now on, all now pensionados will have to pay the same taxes on their automobiles and household goods as ordinary Costa Rican citizens. The rest of the pensionado's privileges remain pretty much intact, the most notable of which is permanent residency whereby you can stay in the country legally. So, we suggest you consider these facts before deciding if it is advantageous for you to become a pensionado.

Despite the apparent short commings of the new law, many retirees will still find Costa Rica an attractive retirement haven since the country has so much to offer. People should continue to flock to Costa Rica because of the peaceful atmosphere, excellent climate, friendly people, natural beauty and so much more that we have mentioned throughout the course of this book, and not because of tax exonerations on a few luxury items. In addition, there is a good chance that the Costa Rican government will reduce some taxes on cars and other formerly taxed imported goods, making them affordable to most Costa Ricans as well as foreign residents, thus eliminating the need for any type of tax exoneration program.

If it is absolutely necessary to have an automobile, you can always bring one from the states, that is five years or older, and only pay a couple of thousand dollars in taxes on it. You can also go to the 'free port' of Golfito in southern Costa Rica, where a stove, refrigerator or other appliances can be purchased without paying high import duties.

Finally, it should be of some comfort to any person thinking about becoming a pensionado that a lawsuit has been filed on behalf of the pensionados, by the Pensionado Association, in response to the elimination of their tax privileges. So, there is some glimmer of hope that this new law will be revoked.

Now we would like to list the requirements and specific documents that you must present to the Costa Rican government if you should choose to apply for either the resident pensionado or resident rentista status. These requirements are subject to change at any given time so check before you start your paperwork.

1. **Resident Pensionado**
   A. A life time income of at least $600 a month generated from outside of Costa Rica.
   B. A signed letter confirming that you will receive this money in Costa Rica.
   C. A letter from a C.P.A. stating that you will receive the $600 for life.
   D. If the money comes from a company, two letters from bank officials showing that your company is financially sound.
   E. A detailed account of your company's pension plan.

2. **Pensionado Rentista**
   A. An income of $1,000 per month for the next five years.
   B. If the income is from a foreign source you need documentation that attests to the company's solvency.

3. **The following other documents are required for both the Pensionado and Rentista categories:**
   A. An application to the Director of Intelligence and Security.
   B. Medical examinations performed by the corresponding departments of the ministry of Public Health of Costa Rica.
   C. The formal application should have the following information: full name, nationality, passport number, dependents, date of entry into Costa Rica, origin of income and the amount, address in country of origin or Costa Rica; authentication by a notary public and corresponding stamps.

4. **A sworn notarized declaration:** Stating that you won't work in Costa Rica; that if you leave the country you will notify I.C.T.; that you will spend 4 months a year in Costa Rica; that you have no police record; that you will change the required number of dollars per month at a national bank.

5. **Police Certificate** from your local area stating that you have no record. (This document is only good for 6 months, so make sure it is current.)

6. **Birth Certificate**

7. **Marriage certificate** if applicable

8. **Certified copy** of your entire passport

9. **Certificate of non-residence**

10. **Twelve passport size photos** - 6 front view and 6 profile

When you have received all the above documents and choose your desired attorney, your attorney should present the proper papers to the tourist board (I.C.T.), who will then process them in about two months.

Should you desire additional information write:

Asociación de Pensionados y Rentistas de Costa Rica
Apartado 700-11011

San José, Costa Rica
Call: 33-80-68 inside Costa Rica and 011-506-33-8068 if you are outside the country.

or contact:

Departamento de Rentistas
Instituto Costarricense de Turismo
Apartado 777-1000
San José, Costa Rica

For a small annual fee ($50), the Pensionado Association *(Asociación de Pensionados y Rentistas)*, located in the ICT building on Avenida 4 at Calle 5 diagonal from the National Theater, will assist you with the following if you need help: applying for residency and pensionado status ($500.00), renewal of Costa Rican I. D. carnet (CEDULA), buying and selling cars, obtaining a Costa Rican driver's license (see page 51 for details), written translations from English into Spanish for important documents, and obtaining medical coverage offered by the Costa Rican Social Security System and the new supplemental coverage offered by the Pensionado Association (see the section on medical care for details).

UPDATE: As of July 1992, the Pensionado Association is being reorganized and to some extent revitalized, and now plans to offer their services to all foreign residents in Costa Rica and not just the pensionados as before.

OTHER IMMIGRATION MATTERS

APPLYING FOR COSTA RICAN RESIDENCY

Since most of the pensionado programs attractive privileges were recently removed, it might be more advantageous to apply for Costa Rican residency. Basically, the residency program is for those people that want to reside in Costa Rica on a full-time basis, but cannot qualify for pensionado status, or those who can qualify, but chose not to do so because some of the benefits that were recently taken away. Besides having to reside six months a year in Costa Rica, foreigners who want to become residents have three ways in which they can acquire residency. They can invest $50,000 in a 'priority project' such as reforestation, tourism, exports, or $200,000 in anything else. They can also claim residency because they have an immediate relative in Costa Rica - a child, spouse or parent or they can prove that they have the financial means to support themselves while living in Costa Rica (about $600 per month).

Because each persons' situation is different, the procedure is complicated and there is a lot of paper work, we advise you to consult a lawyer to facilitate this process. To find a competent, trustworthy attorney, it is best to go to the Pensionado Association office (Association de Pensionados y Rentistas) and read the section in this chapter titled "How to Find a Lawyer."

If you don't want to hassle becoming a pensionado or resident, you can live as a perpetual tourist in Costa Rica. There is no paperwork or lawyers. Just leave the country every three months to renew your visa (tourist card). The only disadvantage is that as a tourist you can't work in Costa Rica and it is almost impossible to become a legal resident, unless you have immediate Costa Rican relatives.

EXTENDING TOURIST CARDS

Every tourist is given permission to remain in Costa Rica for ninety days. To extend their stay, tourists must apply for an extension, called a *PRORROGA*, prior to the end of their first ninety days in the country. A tourist is usually entitled to one of two such extensions, depending on the circumstances of the request. The former immigration offices were located on the east side if the court building, Calle 21, Avenidas 4-6. The new offices are located in the suburb of La Uruca, near the Irazú Hotel and LACSA's main offices. Most travel agencies can help with extending tourist cards and/or exit visas for a small fee. This method will help you avoid long lines and save you valuable time. If you chose not to renew your papers and stay in the country illegally you will have to pay small fine when you eventually do leave.

LEAVING THE COUNTRY

Any tourist who has stayed in Costa Rica for more than thirty days must get a *PENSION ALIMENTICIA* document at the Supreme Court building and an *EXIT VISA* at the immigration office in order to leave the country. Costa Rican citizens, retirees and permanent residents must also do the same. If you are a foreigner, living under one of the three residency categories your resident's exit visa, will costs about $40.00.

CHILDREN'S EXIT VISAS

Children under 18 of all nationalities, even infants, are not allowed to remain in Costa Rica for more than thirty days unless both parents request permission from the National Child Welfare Agency *(Patronato Nacional de la Infancia)* for the child to leave the country. One parent or guardian cannot get permission without written permission from the non-accompanying other parent. This document has to be notarized by a Costa Rican consul in the child's home country. If you don't adhere to this procedure, your child will not be able to leave the country. A travel agent or lawyer may be able to get permission from the Patronato if you give them the child's passport and two extra Costa Rican-sized passport photos.

BRINGING AN AUTOMOBILE TO COSTA RICA

There are two ways to bring a car to Costa Rica - by sea or by land. If you choose to have your car shipped to Costa Rica by boat you should contact a shipping company near to where you have your vehicle in the U.S. or one of the companies we mention in the next section of this book. This method of transportation is relatively safe since your car travels by ship and you can insure it against all types of possible damage. Depending on where you ship your car from in the United States or Canada, your vehicle should not take more than a month to reach Costa Rica, if you have all of your paperwork in order. The cost can range from a few hundred dollars to over a thousand dollars depending on the port of departure. One of the advantages of sending your car this way is that you can sometimes load it with your small household goods so that you won't have to send them separately. Don't forget to inventory and insure these items.

If you have a lot of time on your hands and like adventure, you can drive your automobile to Costa Rica. The journey from the U.S. to Costa Rica, depending on the point along the U.S. Mexican border where you choose to enter, can be made in about three weeks if you drive at a moderate speed. (The shortest distance from the U.S. to Costa Rica by land is 2250 miles through Browsville, Texas). It is best to take your time so that you can stop and see some of the sights. This way you can rest and will only have to drive during the day. We recommend driving during the day since most roads are poorly lighted at night and large animals like cows, donkeys and horses can stray onto the road at anytime and cause a serious accident.

It is important that your car be in good mechanical shape before you undertake your trip. Carry necessary spare tires and parts. You should also have a can of gas and try to keep your gas tank as full as possible since service stations can be few and far between.

Be sure that all your documents such as visas and passports are in order well in advance to avoid problems at border crossings. You also need to have complete car insurance, a valid driver's license and a vehicle registration. If you are missing any of these items, border guards can make your life miserable. It is a good idea to take along some inexpensive gifts from the U.S. such as blank cassettes, or even cash to give to the border police. These "tips" or small bribes help you avoid some delays and may expedite red tape at the borders. Some border crossings close down at night so you should plan to arrive at all borders between 8 a.m. and 5 p.m., just to be safe.

When you finally do arrive at the Costa Rican border from Nicaragua, you may be delayed for some time clearing customs, especially if you are bringing a lot of personal possessions from the U.S. with the intention of living in Costa Rica permanently. Some or all of these items might be inventoried and taken to the custom's warehouse in San José where you can pick them up at a later date, once you have paid the necessary taxes.

It is our understanding that a tourist may keep a car in the country for up to three months. An additional three month extension can be applied for and is usually granted, but after a total of six months the vehicle will have to be taken out of the country or it will be taxed. However, any person who brings a car to Costa Rica by land or sea, and pays all of the taxes, may keep the a car in the country indefinitely once all the necessary paperwork has been completed.

If you do decide that you want to keep your vehicle in Costa Rica, here is a simple formula for figuring out how much you will have to pay in taxes. You pay 100 percent of the value of a new car and 60 percent of the value of a new pickup truck, plus the value of those shipping charges. If the car is a year old, you get a 20% discount. You get a 10% discount for the second, third and fourth years. For example, for a five year old car, you pay taxes on 30% of the value. The value is the manufacturer's suggested retail price. This means if you have a five year old car that is valued at $9,000 and you paid $1,000 to ship it, you owe the customs $3,000.

Those of you who would like additional information on driving from the U.S. to Costa Rica, can purchase a new guide book on the subject by writing: Interlink 209, P.O. Box 526-770 Miami, FL. 33152 if you live outside of Costa Rica. If you currently reside in Costa Rica, you can write to: Ray Prichard, Marketing Consultants, APDO 208-3000, Heredia, Costa Rica, C.A. The price of this book is $13.00 plus $2.50 for postage and handling.

SHIPPING YOUR HOUSEHOLD GOODS TO COSTA RICA

As previously stated, the old pensionado program enabled retirees to import many household items including an automobile virtually duty-free. Since most of these privileges have been rescinded, you might have second thoughts about importing any of said items. You shouldn't worry because many of these goods, or a facsimile can be puchased in Costa Rica. They usually cost more than in the U. S., except at the free port of Golfito in southern Costa Rica, because they are imported. Also, the selection is not nearly as good and the quality of some local items leaves a lot to be desired. So, in some cases it may still be better to purchase your household articles in the U.S. and ship them to Costa Rica by boat, if you can afford to, once you have decided to make Costa Rica your permanent home.

To save time and money, it is best to purchase these goods in Los Angeles, Houston, New Orleans or preferably Miami. The latter is the nearest U.S. port of departure to Costa Rica and shipping costs are even lower. You can look in the yellow pages of the Miami phone book to locate a shipping company or contact one of the companies we have listed below. We understand that there are also some trucking companies that will ship your belongings overland.

It must be pointed out that after taking high shipping costs into consideration, you may be reluctant to ship any household items from the U.S. - this is a matter of personal choice. Most foreign residents and even Costa Ricans prefer U.S. products because of their higher quality. However, not all of household items need to be imported of one is cost conscious and living on a restricted budget or small pension. Many retirees live comfortably and happily without some or any luxuries and expensive appliances. What you need to import really depends on your personal lifestyle and budget.

Here are some money saving tips for bringing your household goods to Costa Rica. First, if you enter the country as a tourist by plane, you can usually bring in a lot of personal effects and small appliances. As a tourist sometimes you are even waved through customs without ever having to open any of your luggage. You can also have friends bring a few things to you when they visit you in Costa Rica. Any way you look at it, you should always try to take as much with you as you can by plane rather than shipping items by boat, because most used personal items are not taxed at the airport. Even used appliances have a good chance of clearing airport customs if you can fit them on the plane. You should make an effort to get rid of 'clutter' and not ship anything that you can easily and cheaply replace in Costa Rica. You should also make a point of talking to other retirees to find out what they think is absolutely necessary and not necessary to bring to Costa Rica.

If you chose to send some of your possessions by ship, once they arrive in Costa Rica you will have to excercise extreme patience and be prepared to face many unnecessary delays and frustrating situations when dealing with the Costa Rican custom's house or *aduana* as it is called. It is not unusual to have to make many trips to the custom's warehouse to get your belongings. You may spend all day going from window to window and dealing with mountains of paperwork, only to be told at the end of the day that you have to come the following morning to pick up your belongings. Futhermore, fickle customs officials decide the value of the shipped goods and two shipments exactly the same, can have completely different tax amounts, depending who examines them at the aduana.

Because of this dilatory process, many people pay a local customs broker, *Agencia Aduanera*, or hire some other person like their lawyer to do this unpleasent task for them. It may cost you a little more this way, but it will save you valuable time. For additional information contact by phone or write:

Worldwide Movers Air and Sea Freight
P.O. Box 253-1007
Centro Colón
San José, Costa Rica
Fax (506) 33-0517
Tel: 011-506-33-4785
Servex Inernational S.A.
P.O.Box 1285-1000
San José, Costa Rica
Tel: 011-506-53-1152
Fax 506-24-8437

Consult the yellow pages for listing of Agencias Aduaneras (Custom's brokers). The Pensionado Association suggests you contact moving expert, Carlos Bravo before you decide to ship your belongings to Costa Rica. Tel: 53-11-52, Fax: 24-84-37.

HOW TO FIND A LAWYER

If you plan to go into business, work, buy or sell property and/or seek long term residence status, you will certainly need the services of a good attorney. Your attorney can also help you understand the complexities of the Costa Rican legal system, which is based on Roman law and does not work like our system in the United States, assist you with bureaueratic procedures and handle any other legal matters that might arise.

As you already know, the lawyer you chose as well as his secretary should be bilingual (Spanish/English). This will help you avoid communication problems, misunderstandings, and enables you to stay on top of your legal affairs. It is very important to watch your lawyer closely, since most Costa Rican lawyers tend to drag their feet like bureaucrats. Never take for granted that things are getting done. Check with your lawyer on a regular basis and ask to see your file to make sure he has taken care of you business. As you know paper work is slow moving in Costa Rica, and you don't want to protract the process any more than you have to. Also, be sure that your lawyer is accessible at all hours. You should have his office telephone number and his home number in case you have to locate him if there is an emergency. If your lawyer is always in meetings or out of the office this is a clear sign that your work is being neglected and you have chosen the wrong lawyer. You should also make sure that you know your lawyer's specialty. Although most attorneys are required to have a general knowledge of Costa Rican law, you may need a specialist to deal with your specific case. Some retirees have found is a good idea to have several lawyers for precisely this reason.

It is best to take your time and look around when you are trying to find a good lawyer. Ask other retirees and knowledgeable people for the names of their lawyers, and then try to find out as much as you can about your potential lawyer's reputation and how he works. If you find yourself in a jam, you can contact the Pensionado Association or go to one of the many lawyer's offices located in the vicinity of the courthouse. Like everywhere else in the world, there are always some incompetent, unscrupulous attorneys, so it is best to know who you are dealing with before you make you final choice. Remember, one of the most important people you will be associated with while living in Costa Rica is your lawyer, so it is of utmost importance that you develop a good working relationship.

It is not advisable to select a lawyer solely on the basis of legal fees. Lawyers fees, or *honorarios,* vary and just because a lawyer charges a lot doesn't mean he is good. Likewise you shouldn't choose an attorney because his fees are low. However, if you can find a competent lawyer who will handle your pensionado paperwork for under $500.00 you are getting a good deal. You can check with the Costa Rican equivalent of the Bar Association *(El Colegio de Abogados)* if you have any questions about legal fees.

You will be happy to know that in Costa Rica it is surprisingly more affordable than you think to hire a lawyer on a full time basis, by paying what amounts to a small retainer. You should also know that there is a small amount of paper work involved to give your lawyer "power of attorney" *poder* so he or she can take care of your personal business and legal affairs. This is not a bad idea if you ever have to leave the country for a period of time or in the event of an emergency. However, first make sure your lawyer is completely trustworthy and competent in such matters.

COSTA RICAN CONSULATES AND EMBASSIES ABROAD

Anyone who wants to become a pensionado or seeks permanent residency in Costa Rica will have to have certain documents notarized by a Costa Rican consulate or embassy in their country of origin. Some if the documents that may need to be notarized are: a birth certificate, police certificate (stating you have no criminal record) and proof of income statement. It is recommended that all this paper work be taken care of before coming to Costa Rica. If you apply for any type of permanent residency status from Costa Rica it may take months for you to get the required notarized documents from your home country. If worse comes to worse you may even have to make an unnecessary trip home to take care of these matters. Also, while you are waiting for your papers from abroad some of the other documents may expire and you will have to go through the process all over again. Bureaucracy is slow enough as it is in Costa Rica, and it is foolish to delay this process any more than necessary.

Here are some of the Costa Rican Consulates and Embassies abroad:

Consulates in the United States:

Los Angeles	Miami	New Orleans
1343 West Olympic Blvd.	28 W. Flager St.	2 Canal Street
Los Angeles, Ca. 90015	Miami, Fl. 33130	New Orleans, La. 70130
New York	Chicago	Dallas
S. Wall Street	8 S. Michigan Ave.	4200 Repub. Bank Tower
New York, NY 10005	Chicago, Ill. 60603	Dallas, Tx. 75201

Embassies:

United States	Canada	England
1825 Connecticut Ave. NW	14 Lancaster Gate	150 Argyle Street
Washington DC, 20009	London	Ottawa, Ontario
	K2P 1B7	W2 3LH

EMBASSIES AND CONSULATES IN COSTA RICA

If you are planning to travel and explore Latin America and other parts of the world, once you are settled in Costa Rica, you will need the addresses of the embassies and consulates listed below in order to get visas and other necessary travel documents.

Argentina, Ave 6 Calle 21-25 21-34-38
Austria (consulate) Ave. 2 Calle 2-4 23-28-22
Belgium, Los Yoses 25-03-51
Bolivia, Ave Central, Calle 4-6 22-52-68
Brazil, Ave. ct 1. Calle 4 33-15-44
Canada, Ave ct. 1 Calle 3 23-04-46
Columbia, Ave. 5 Calle 5 21-07-25
Chile, Barrio Dent 24-42-43
China, San Pedro 24-81-80
Ecuador (consulate) Calles 40-42, Ave. 2 22-14-49
El Salvador, Los Yoses 25-58-87
France, Curridabat 25-07-33
Great Britain, Centro Colón 21-55-66
Germany, Rohrmoser 32-55-33
Guatemala, Colonia del Rio 22-21-45
Honduras, Ave 2-4, Calles 1-3 22-21-45
Italy, Los Yoses 24-65-74
Israel, Ave, 2-4, Calle 2 21-60-11
Jamaica (consulate) Urb. Los Anonos 28-08-02
Japan, Rohrmoser 32-12-55
Mexico, Ave. 7, Calles 5-7 33-88-74
Nicaragua, Barrio California........................33-92-25
Panama, San Pedro 25-34-01
Paraguay, Los Yoses 25-69-91
Peru, Calle 4, Ave. Ctl 22-56-44
Spain, Calle 30/32, Paseo Colón 22-19-33
United States of America:, Rohrmoser 20-39-39
Uruguay, Calle 2, Ave. 1.......................................23-25-12
Venezuela, Los Yoses 25-88-10

PART NINE

Other Useful

Information

COSTA RICA'S POTABLE WATER

Unlike other countries in Latin America, especially Mexico, Costa Rica's water supply is good and perfectly safe to drink in San José and in the majority of small towns. In most places, you can drink water without fear of "Montezuma's Revenge" (dysentery) or other intestinal problems. However, be careful when you drink water in the countryside. We have lived in Costa Rica for years and not heard many people complain about the quality of Costa Rica's water. But if you prefer, bottled water is available. You will be pleased to know that Costa Rica's water is also soft for bathing purposes.

FRUITS, VEGETABLES AND OTHER BARGAIN FOODS

There is a wide variety of delicious tropical fruits and vegetables in Costa Rica. As a matter of fact it is amazing that there is every imaginable fruit and vegetable you can think of plus some exotic native varieties. More common tropical fruits such as pineapples, mangos, and papayas cost about a third of what they do in the United States. Bananas can be purchased at any local fruit stand or street market for about five cents each.

Once you have lived in Costa Rica you can do like many Costa Ricans and eat a few slices of mouth-watering fruit for breakfast at one of the many sidewalk *fruterías* or fruit stands located all over the country. For people who are living on a tight budget, this type of healthy fresh-fruit breakfast will cost you about 50 or 60 cents. There are also many *sodas*, or small, traditional cafes, where you can eat a more typical Costa Rican breakfast for around a dollar.

Besides fruits and vegetables there are many other bargain foods available in Costa Rica. Bakeries sell fresh home-made breads and pastries. We recommend the Schmidt chain of bakeries. Other foods such as eggs, chicken, meats, cheeses and honey etc...are available at most small neighborhood grocery stores, *pulperías* as well as large supermarkets. These supermarkets are much like markets in the states in that they have everything under one roof, but differ because they don't have the selection or number of products found in the average U.S. market.

Many prepackaged imported products can be found in Costa Rican supermarkets but are very expensive. It is not unusual to pay double for a box of your favorite breakfast cereal, certain canned foods or liquor. You don't have to worry because there are some local products that you can substitute for your favorite U.S. brand. However, if you find that you absolutely cannot live without your prepackaged foods from the states, you can usually find the product you are looking for at Bubis' imported food stores or at one of the Auto Mercados supermarkets at a very high price. If you want to save money, we suggest that you stock-up on these items while on a shopping trip to the states, and bring them with you by plane when you return to Costa Rica. You can also have friends or relatives bring you the food items you need when they visit you. If you ever go to the neighboring country of Panama you can find many American food products sold there.

Since most foods are so affordable in Costa Rica, you will be better off if you try changing your eating habits and buy more local products and substitutes so you can keep your food bill low. You can further save money by shopping at the Central Market, *Mercado Central* , like many cost-conscious Costa Ricans. The market covers a whole city block and is located in the heart of downtown San José, near the banking district. Everything is under one roof and there are hundreds of shops where you can buy fresh fruits, vegetables, grains and much more. You can also go to one of the open-air street markets, called *ferias del agricultor*, on any Saturday morning. Farmers bring their fresh produce to these street markets each week, and you can find a variety of produce, meats and eggs at low prices.

A few words about Costa Rica's excellent seafood. With oceans on both sides, Costa Rica has a huge variety of fresh seafood. Tuna, dorado, corvina, abound as well as lobster, shrimp of all sizes and some crab. All of these can be purchased at any *Pescadería* (fish market) in and around San José's Central Market at low prices. While you're there, try a heaping plate of *Ceviche* (fish cocktail) at one of the many fish restaurants called *Marisquerías*.

Typical Costa Rican Food is similar to that of Mexico and other Central American Countries. Tortillas often but not always are eaten with a meal of rice, beans, fruit, eggs vegetables and a little meat. The most common dish, *Gallo Pinto* is made from rice and black beans and fried with red bell peppers and cilantro. The best gallo pinto is served at La Soda Tapia restaurant opposite the Savana Park in San José.

Some other popular Costa Rican foods include: *Casado* (fish, chicken, or meat with beans and chopped cabbage), *empanadas* (a type of stuffed bread), *arreglados* (a kind of sandwich) and *palmito* (heart of palm), which is usually eaten separately or in salads.

MAJOR SUPERMARKETS

PERIFERICOS (several locations in the San José area)

MAS POR MENOS (largest chain)

AUTO MERCADOS (the best supermarkets in Costa Rica)

LA GRAN VIA (downtown San José)

BUBIS (specializing in expensive imported food products)

PALI SUPERMERCADOS (discount warehouses)

CENTRAL MARKET - MERCADO CENTRAL, located between Avenida Central and 1 and calle 6 and 8, has great food bargains, as we mention above.

RELIGION

Although 90% of Costa Ricans are Roman Catholic, there is freedom of religion and other religious views are permitted. We hope the list we have provided below will help you. Call the number of your denomination and you will be directed to your nearest house of worship in the San José area. There are some services in English in the San José area. (The asterics denote churches where these special services in English are held).

```
* QUAKER ...................................................................... 33-61-68
  UNITARIAN ............................................ 28-10-20 or 28-41-96
  SYNAGOGUE SHAARE ZION (Jewish) ................... 22-54-49
* B'NAI ISRAEL ........................................................ 25-85-61
  PROTESTANT ......................................................... 28-05-53
* UNION CHURCH ..................................................... 26-36-70
  MORMAN ........................................... 22-98-58 or 33-44-58
  YOGA ....................................................................... 21-58-95
  METHODIST .......................................................... 22-03-60
  CHRISTIAN SCIENCE ............................................ 21-08-40
* BAPTIST (San Pedro) ................................................ 53-79-11
  EPISCOPAL ............................................................ 22-15-08
* ESCAZU CHRISTIAN FELLOWSHIP ..................... 32-14-07
  JEHOVAH'S WITNESS ........................................... 21-14-36
  SEVENTH DAY ADVENTISTS ........... 25-06-65 or 24-83-44
* CATHOLIC (ESCAZU) ............................................. 28-06-35
  CATHOLIC (LOS YOSES) ...................................... 25-67-78
  CATHOLIC (ROHRMOSER) .................................. 32-21-28
  CATHOLIC (BARRIO SAN BOSCO) ...................... 21-37-48
  CATHOLIC (DOWNTOWN CATHEDRAL) ............. 21-38-20
* EPISCOPAL CHURCH OF THE GOOD SHEPHERD ............. 22-15-60
* VICTORY CHRISTIAN CENTER ............................ 82-77-20
* UNITY CHRIST INTERNATIONAL ...................... 28-68-05
```

HOLIDAYS IN COSTA RICA

Costa Ricans are very nationalistic and proudly celebrate their official holidays, called *Feriados*. You should try to plan your activities around these holidays and not count on getting any important bureacratic matters or business done since most government and private offices will be closed on some of the following days.

January 1st	NEW YEAR'S DAY
January 15th	SANTA CRUZ FIESTAS
March 19th	SAINT JOSEPH'S DAY
March	DIA DEL BOYERO (Oxcart Driver Day)
Holy Week	HOLY THURSDAY and GOOD FRIDAY
April 11th	JUAN SANTA MARIA'S DAY (local hero)
April 21st	ROMERIA (pilgimage)
May 1st	LABOR DAY
May	UNIVERSITY WEEK
June	FATHER'S DAY (third Sunday)
July 25th	ANNEXATION OF GUANACASTE PROVINCE
August 2nd	VIRGIN OF LOS ANGELES DAY
August 15th	MOTHER'S DAY
Saptember 15th	INDEPENDENCE DAY
October 12th	COLUMBUS DAY - Discovery of America
October 12th	LIMON CARNIVAL
October 31st	HALLOWEEN
November 2nd	DAY OF THE DEAD
December 8th	IMMACULATE CONCEPTION
December 25th	CHRISTMAS
December 25th	FERIA DE ZAPOTE (December 25th to January 2nd)
December 25th	FIESTAS DEL FIN DEL AÑO

TRAPICHE - SUGAR MILL

BRINGING YOUR PETS TO COSTA RICA

We did not forget those of you who have pets. There are procedures for bringing your pets into the country that require very little except patience, some paperwork and a small fee.

First, a registered veterinarian from your home town must certify that your pets are free of internal and external parasites. It is necessary that your pet's vaccinations are up to date against rabies, distemper, leptosporosis, hepatitis and parvovirus with the rabies vaccination within the last three years. Remember, all of these required documents are indispensable and must be certified also by the Costa Rican consulate nearest your home town.

Now if you should forget to comply with these regulations and not provide the required documents your pet(s) can be refused entry, placed in quarantine or even put to sleep. But don't worry if worse come to worse there is a 30 day grace period to straighten things out.

If you ever want to take your pet out of Costa Rica you will have to get a special permit. You will also need a certificate from a local veterinarian and have all vacinations up-to-date. Once you obtain thise documents, you then have to go to the Ministry of Health, and your pet is free to leave the country.

Additional information and the requirements listed above are available through the Departamento de Zoonosis, Ministerio de Salud, Apartado Postal 10123, San José. Telephone 23-03-33, extension 331.

VETERINARIANS

Clinica Echandi	23-31-11
Dr. Federico Piza	48-71-66
Dr. Douglas Lutz	25-67-84
Dr. L. Starkey	53-71-42
Tecnologia Veterinaria (clinic, pharmacy, and boarding)	28-93-47

For additional Veterinarians, look under the heading *"VETERINARIA"* in the yellow pages.

DOG GROOMING

Marie Dog - stylist	25-38-05

PART TEN

Parting Thoughts
and Advice

PERSONAL SAFETY IN COSTA RICA

While living in Costa Rica is much safer than residing in any large city in the United States or most other Latin American countries, there are some precautions you should take to insure your own safety. In Costa Rica, the rate for violent crimes is very low when compared with other places in the world, but there is a lot of theft, especially in the larger cities. Thieves tend to look for easy targets, above all foreigners, so you can't be too cautious. We recommend that you make sure that your house or apartment has steel bars on both the windows and garage. These bars should be narrowly spaced, because some thieves have been known to use small children as accomplices in order to have them squeeze through the bars and burglarize your residence. It is also a good idea to make sure your neighborhood has a night watchman if you live in the city. Some male domestic employees will be willing to work in this capacity. However, you should ask for references and closely screen any person you hire to avoid theft. Also, report suspicious people that may be loitering around your premises. Thieves are very patient and will often case a residence for a long time observing your comings and goings, so that they can strike at the most opportune moment.

You should take added precautions if you live in a neighborhood where there are a lot of foreigners. Thieves associated foreigners with wealth and look for areas where foreigners are clustered together. One possible deterrent, in addition to a night watchman, is to organize some type of neighborhood watch group among the residents of your area. There are also private home security patrols that will provide an alarm system and patrol your area for a monthly fee. If you have to leave town it is also a good idea to get a friend or some other trustworthy person to housesit while you are away. If you are really concerned about protecting your valuables, you will be better off living in a condominium complex or an apartment. Both tend to be less susceptible to burglary due to their design and the fact that there is usually more "safety in numbers", as the saying goes.

If you own an automobile, you should also be careful, especially if you have pensionado (retiree) license plates. These plates identify you as a foreigner and in some cases make you a sitting duck for car burglars who relish the opportunity to break into your car and steal your valuables. Also, make sure that your house or apartment has a garage with iron bars so you don't have to park your car on the street. When parking away from your house, you should always park in the parking lots or where there is a watchman. The latter will look after your car for a few cents an hour when you have to park it on the street. It is not difficult to find one of these people to watch your car since they will usually approach you and offer their services as soon as you park your car.

Pickpockets can be a problem. You should never flaunt your wealth by wearing expensive jewelry or carrying cameras because they also make you an easy mark on the street. Also you should find a good way to conceal your money and never carry it in your back pocket. If you have to carry large amounts of money it is best to use traveller's checks. You should also never carry any original documents, such as passports or visas. Make a photocopy of your passport and carry it with you at all times. The authorities will accept most photocopies as a valid form of identification. Men should also watch out for prostitutes, who often are expert pickpockets and can relieve you of your valuables without you even realizing it. Men, especially when inebriated or alone, should watch themselves at night in the vicinity of Morazán Park, The Holiday Inn and Key Largo Bar. There have been a lot of muggings reported in this area at night.

If you are a single woman living by yourself, you should never walk alone at night. In the event that you do have to go out at night, be sure to take a taxi or have a friend go along.

There is some white collar crime in Costa Rica and many dishonest individuals waiting to take your money. We have heard countless horror stories of naive foreigners losing their hard earned savings to con men's scams. So, be wary of business deals that seem too good to be true or any "get rich quick" schemes. Most people you meet in Costa Rica will be honest, hard-working individuals. But don't assume people are honest just because they are nice. Again, it doesn't hurt to be overly cautious.

If you are robbed or swindled under any circumstances you should contact the police or in some cases the *O.I.J.* (**Organización de Investigación Judicial** - a special, highly efficient investigative unit like the FBI). You may not recover what has been stolen from you, but you may prevent others from being victimized in the future.

CONCLUSION

Throughout this book we have attempted to provide you with the most up to date information available on retirement and living in Costa Rica. We have also given you many useful suggestions that can help to make your life in Costa Rica more enjoyable and save you a lot of inconveniences since adjusting to life in a new culture can prove rather difficult for some people. One of our aims is to make this transition easier, so that you can take advantage of all the marvelous things that Costa Rica has to offer. We highly recommend that before you move permanently to Costa Rica, you spend some time there on a trial basis to make sure that it is indeed the place for you. We are not talking about a few days or weeks, but a couple of months or even longer, so that you can experience what Costa Rican life is really like. You should remember that it is one thing to visit Costa Rica as a tourist and another thing to live there on a permanent basis. It is also best that you go there for extended visits during both the wet season, as well as the dry season. This way you can get an idea of what the country is like at all times of the year. During your visits you should talk to as many foreign retirees as you can and gather as much information as possible before you make your final decision. Also, it is a good idea to attend one of the Newcomer's Seminars that take place the second Tuesday of every month at the Irazú Hotel. They are very informative and you can learn a lot by talking to other retirees and make some good contacts.

The final step, that you might want to take before deciding if you want to make Costa Rica your home, is to try living there for at least a year. This should be sufficient time to give you an idea of what long-term living in Costa Rica is really like and the kind of problems you will be confronted with while trying to adapt to living in a new culture. It should also afford you the opportunity to get acclimated to the climate and new foods. Hopefully you should learn all the do's and don'ts, in's and out's and places to go and places to avoid during the period of time, so that you can make your final decision.

If you do chose to reside in Costa Rica on a full time basis, here are some things that you should keep in mind regarding the cultural differences and new customs you will be encountering. First, life in Costa Rica is very different and if you expect all things to be exactly like they are in the United States, you are deceiving yourself. For example, as we have already alluded to earlier in this book, the concept of time and punctuality is not that important in Latin America. It is not unusual and not considered in bad taste for a person to arrive late for a business appointment or a dinner engagement. This custom can be incomprehensible and infuriating to the North American mentality but cannot be changed since it is a deeply rooted tradition. Also, as we previously mentioned, in most cases bureaucracy moves at a snail's pace in Costa Rica, which can be equally maddening to a foreigner. In addition, at times, the Latin mentality, machismo, apparent illogical reasoning, traditions, different laws and ways of doing business, can seem incomprehensible to a naive foreigner.

There are countless other examples of different customs and cultural idiosyncrasies that you will notice once you have lived in Costa Rica for a while. The best thing you can do is to respect these different cultural values, be understanding, patient, and as they say "go with the flow". Learning Spanish will help you achieve this end to some degree. Finally, you shouldn't burn your bridges as they say, or sever your ties with your home country in the event that you cannot adjust to life in Costa Rica and decide to return home.

Despite our efforts to constantly update this book, all of the aforementioned data may be subject to change at any given time. So, "THE GOLDEN DOOR TO RETIREMENT AND LIVING IN COSTA RICA" urges you to be sure and check and see that our information is still accurate. . .

THANK YOU!

ADDITIONAL RETIREMENT INFORMATION

COSTA RICAN TRAVEL ADVISORS offers chartered, escorted retirement tours and regular excursions around San José and the rest of the country in a luxurious, air conditioned Greyhound bus. This is one of the best and safest ways to see Costa Rica. Their bus has half the number of seats as a regular bus and is therefore very spacious and comfortable. The company's motto is "See Costa Rica and Leave the Driving to Us." We highly recommend this company since they also arrange hotel reservations, fishing excursions, provide tourist information and many other tourist related services. They have a desk conveniently located in the lobby of the Dunn Inn, in downtown San José. For addition information contact:

Costa Rican Travel Advisors
P.O. Box 896-1250
Escazú, Costa Rica, or
TEL. (506) 22-81-34 or 28-08-67
FAX (506) 21-45-96

The *COSTA RICAN OUTLOOK* is an innovative, bi-monthly newsletter that covers a wide range of subjects and is packed with useful information about Costa Rica including an occasional article about retirement. Reading this newsletter is another good way to keep abrest of what is happening in Costa Rica. You can subscribe for $19.00 a year if you live in the U.S. and $22.00 outside the U.S. Write: *Costa Rican Outlook*
P.O. Box 5573
Chula Vista, CA 91912-5573

The *PEN/REN NEWS* is published by the Pensionado Association and not for sale to the general public. However, if you join the Pensionado Association your membership will include a monthly copy of their newsletter. For information:

Asosciación de Pensionados y Rentistas de Costa Rica
Apdo. Postal 700 1011
Y Griega
San José, Costa Rica
Central America
TEL. (506) 33-80-68 & 33-10-17
FAX (506) 22-78-62

The *NEWCOMER'S SEMINAR* provideds useful information at no charge. These seminars are held each Tuesday at the Hotel Irazú, except the last Tuesday of every month when they are held at the Hotel Cariari. For information:

The Newcomer's Seminar
Box 962
San José, Costa Rica
TEL. (506) 32-13-55
FAX (506) 31-04-69

SUGGESTED READING

The New Key to Costa Rica, by Beatrice Blake. The Bookpeople, Berkeley, California

Costa Rica, A Natural Destination, by Ree Strange Sheck. John Muir Publications, Santa Fe, NM

Costa Rica, by Paul Glassman. Passport Press, Box 1346, Champlain, New York, 12919

Mexico and Central America Handbook. Distributed by Rand McNally.

South America Handbook. Published yearly by Rand McNally.

The Costa Rican Traveler, by Ellen Searby. Windham Bay Press, Box 1198, Occidental CA 95465

Choose Latin America, by John Howells. Gateway Books, San Francisco, CA 94109

Living in Costa Rica, by the U. S. Mission Association

The Tico Times Newspaper. Published weekly. See page 35 for subscription details.

Costa Rica - A Travel Survival Kit, by Rob Rackowiecki. Lonely Planet Publications, Inc., P.O. 2001A, Berkeley, CA 94702.

Central America on a Shoestring, by Geoff Crowther, Lonely Planet Publications, Australia.

The Costa Ricans, by Richards, Karen, and Mavis Biesanz. Waveland Press, Prospect Heights, IL.

Costa Rica Today Newspaper, published weekly. See page 35 for subscription details.

INDEX